FREDERICK II

FREDERICK II

The Wonder of the World

Richard Bressler

WESTHOLME
Yardley

Frontispiece: Emperor Frederick II enthroned. From the Exultet Rolls of Salerno.

Westholme Publishing, LLC
904 Edgewood Road
Yardley, Pennsylvania 19067
Visit our Web site at www.westholmepublishing.com

First Printing July 2010
10 9 8 7 6 5 4 3 2 1

ISBN: 978-1-59416-109-4

Printed in United States of America.

To my parents,
thank you for all your support.

CONTENTS

LIST OF MAPS

List of Principal Persons

Adalasia of Sardinia: Princess of Sardinia, wife of Enzio, Frederick's illegitmate son

Adrian IV: Pope (1154–1159)

Alexander III: Pope (1159–1181)

Al-Kamil: Ruler of Egypt at time of Frederick's crusade

Al-Malik: Ruler of Syria, brother of al-Kamil

Analectus II: Antipope against Innocent II (1130–1138)

Ansaldus di Mari: Genoese seaman, admiral of Sicily for Frederick

Azzo d'este: Ruler of Vicenza, opponent of Ezzelino, son-in-law of Frederick

Barbarossa: see Frederick I

Beatrice of Hohenstaufen: Cousin of Frederick, wife of Otto IV

Beatrice of Savoy: Wife of Manfred, illegitimate son of Frederick

Beatrix of Burgundy: Wife of Barbarossa

Berard of Palermo: Archbishop, close adviser to Frederick

Bernardo Orlando Rossi: Conspirator against Frederick

Bianca Lancia: Mother of Manfred and Constance, long-time lover of Frederick

Cardinal Giovanni Colonna: Ally of Frederick

Cardinal James of Palestrina: Opponent of Frederick

Cardinal Nicholas of Ostia: Opponent of Frederick

Cardinal Ottaviano Degli Ubaldini: Opponent of Frederick

Cardinal Otto of St. Nicholas: Ally of Frederick

Cardinal Rainer of Viterbo: Opponent of Frederick

Cardinal Robert of Somercote: Ally of Frederick

Celestine III: Pope (1191–1198)

Celestine IV: Pope for seventeen days in 1241

Charles of Anjou: Brother of Louis IX of France, conqueror of Manfred and Kingdom of Sicily

Conrad: Son of Frederick and Isabella of Jerusalem, king of Jerusalem, later Holy Roman emperor

Conrad III: Holy Roman emperor (1137–1152), uncle of Barbarossa

Conrad of Thuringia: Successor to Hermann von Salza as head of Teutonic Knights

Conradin: Son of Conrad, grandson of Frederick

Constance of Aragon: Daughter of Manfred, queen of Aragon

Constance of Aragon: First wife to Frederick, married in 1209

Constance of Sicily: Heiress of Kingdom of Sicily, mother of Frederick II

Count of Caserta: Son-in-law, conspirator against Frederick

Count Thomas of Acerra: Noble in the Holy Land, aide to Frederick on crusade

Dipold of Acerra: Associate of Markward

Duke Frederick of Austria: Duke of Austria, opponent of Frederick

Duke William of Aquitaine: Ruler of Aquitaine in twelfth century

Elias of Cortona: Minister-general of Franciscan order

Emir Fakhr Ad-Din: Ambassador from al-Kamil to Frederick

Enzio: Illegitimate son of Frederick, king of Sardinia, military leader for Frederick

Eugenius III: Pope (1145–1154)

Ezzelino da Romano: Ruler of Verona, ally and son-in-law of Frederick

Frederick I (Barbarossa): Holy Roman emperor (1152–1189), grandfather of Frederick

Frederick II of Hohenstaufen: King of Sicily (1198–1250), Holy Roman emperor (1212–1250)

Frederick of Antioch: Illegitimate son of Frederick, representative in the Holy Land

Giovanni il Moro: Successor to Richard as master chamberlain

Gregorio di Montelongo: Clerical opponent of Frederick

Gregory VIII: Pope in 1187

Gregory IX: Pope (1227–1241)

Henry (The Lion): Ruler of Saxony

Henry II of England: King of England (1154–1189), married to Eleanor of Aquitaine

Henry III of England: King of England (1216-1272), brother of Isabella of England

Henry Lusignan: King of Cyprus as minor, at time of Frederick's crusade

Henry of Burgundy: Duke of Burgundy

Henry of Hohenstaufen (The Elder): Son of Frederick and Constance of Aragon

Henry of Hohenstaufen (The Younger): Son of Frederick and Isabella of England

Henry Raspe: Regent for Conrad, then opponent of Frederick

Henry VI: Holy Roman emperor (1189–1197), father of Frederick II

Hermann von Salza: Grand master of Teutonic Knights, adviser to Frederick

Honorius II: Pope (1124–1130)

Honorius III: Pope (1216–1227)

Innocent II: Pope (1130–1143)

Innocent III: Pope (1198–1216), guardian of Frederick (1198–1206)

Innocent IV: Pope (1243–1254)

Isabella of England: Third wife of Frederick, married in 1235

Isabella (Yolande) of Jerusalem: Heiress of Kingdom of Jerusalem, second wife of Frederick, married in 1225

John of Brienne: Titular king of Jerusalem, father of Isabella, opponent of Frederick

John of England: King of England (1199–1216)

John Vatatzes: Son-in-law of Frederick, Greek emperor

Leopold of Austria: Duke of Austria

Liupold: Bishop of Worms, leader of military forces for Philip of Swabia

Lothair of Saxony: Holy Roman emperor (1127–1137)

Louis VII of France: King of France (1137–1180)

Louis VIII of France: King of France (1223–1226)

Louis IX of France: King of France (1226-1270), later St. Louis

Ludwig, Duke of Bavaria: Ruler of Bavaria, regent for Henry of Hohenstaufen

Manfred: Illegitimate son of Frederick and Bianca, successor to Frederick in Kingdom of Sicily

Manuel I: Byzantine emperor (1143–1180)

Margrave of Meissen: Prince in Germany, son-in-law to Frederick

Markward of Anweiler: Seneschal to Henry VI, major force in Kingdom of Sicily (1197–1202)

Matteo Orsini: Senator of Rome, secular ruler of Rome in 1241

Otto IV: Duke of Brunswick, then Holy Roman emperor (1198–1212)

Otto of Wittlesbach: Ruler of Bavaria

Paschal III: Antipope against Alexander (1164–1177)

Pedro of Aragon: Husband of Constance, king of Aragon

Philip II Augustus: King of France (1179–1223)

Philip of Swabia: Duke of Swabia, uncle of Frederick

Piero della Vigna: Logothete of Sicily, civil aide to Frederick

Qadi of Nablus: Muslim leader, host to Frederick in Jerusalem

Rainald of Spoleto: Sicilian noble, military leader under Frederick

Richard: Master chamberlain to Frederick

Richard I (The Lion-Hearted) of England: King of England (1189–1199)

Richard of Cornwall: Brother-in-law to Frederick

Richard of Theate: Illegitimate son of Frederick

Robert Guiscard: Son of Tancred, Norman knight, founder of Sicilian kingdom

Roger I of Sicily: Duke of Sicily until 1101

Roger II of Sicily: Duke, then king of Sicily (1112–1154), grandfather of Frederick

St. Elizabeth of Thuringia: Wife of Margrave of Thuringia, canonized in 1235

Taddeo da Suessa: Clerical ally of Frederick

Tancred of Hauteville: Norman knight, founder of House of Hauteville

Tancred, Count of Lecce: Illegitimate son of William I, king of Sicily in opposition to Henry VI (1189–1194)

Urban II: Pope (1088–1099)

Urban IV: Pope (1254–1264)

Victor IV: Antipope against Alexander (1159–1164)

Walter of Pelear: Chancellor of Kingdom of Sicily, member of Regency Council

Walter of Brienne: French knight, opponent of Markward

William Capparone: Associate of Markward, unofficial guardian of Frederick (1201–1206)

William I (The Bad): King of Sicily (1154–1166), brother of Constance of Sicily

William II (The Good): King of Sicily (1166–1189)

William of Apulia: Cousin of Roger II, duke of Apulia

William of Holland: Duke of Holland, opponent of Frederick

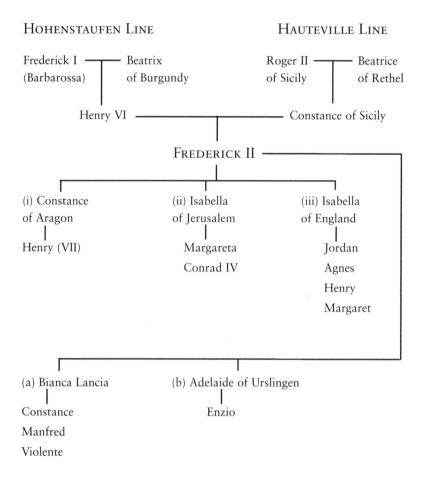

HOHENSTAUFEN LINE   HAUTEVILLE LINE

Frederick I ——— Beatrix   Roger II ——— Beatrice
(Barbarossa)   of Burgundy   of Sicily   of Rethel

Henry VI ———————————— Constance of Sicily

FREDERICK II ———

(i) Constance   (ii) Isabella   (iii) Isabella
of Aragon   of Jerusalem   of England

Henry (VII)   Margareta   Jordan
                  Conrad IV   Agnes

                               Henry

                               Margaret

(a) Bianca Lancia   (b) Adelaide of Urslingen

Constance   Enzio

Manfred

Violente

The family tree of Frederick II. Roman numerals indicate the legitimate wives of Frederick II in order; the lower case letters indicate mistresses with no order indicated. Frederick had a number of other mistresses and illegitimate children not shown on this tree.

PREFACE

As an avid reader of medieval European history, I kept coming across the name and story of Emperor Frederick II of the Holy Roman Empire in various histories of medieval Europe. I also heard Frederick discussed on various science programs as being a forerunner in the discipline of modern animal science, as recorded in his book, *The Art of Falconry*. The small sections about him in these histories and the mentions about his relationship with science fascinated me, and led me to look up more about this person who lived eight hundred years ago.

When I tried to find biographies of Frederick, I came up with many references to him, but only a small selection of biographies in English. I have read these, and note four fine, scholarly ones: *Frederick II: A Medieval Emperor*, by David Abulafia, published in 1988; *The Emperor Frederick II of Hohenstaufen*, by T.C. Van Cleve, 1972; *Frederick II of Hohenstaufen*, by Georgina Masson, 1973; and *Frederick the Second, 1194–1250*, by Ernst Kantorowicz, translated by E.O. Lorimer, 1957.

In this book, I am not competing with these biographies. I decided to write this account of Frederick II to provide a less-annotated, more-condensed version of his life for the general reader in order to bring this fascinating personality to a larger audience. I do not present new information by researching additional primary sources; rather I have taken existing information and tried to put together what I think is a very interesting story of a life lived in the thirteenth century in a Europe much different from that of today. Where the sources disagree, I attempt to compare them to determine what may have occurred.

One of the founders of Western literature, Dante Alighieri, was clearly fascinated by Frederick. He mentions him repeatedly in the *Divine Comedy*. He also wrote a short work, *De Monarchia*, which has a great deal of commentary on the attempt of Frederick to found and rule a world empire, and Frederick's relationship with the Roman Catholic Church that arose from that. Dante was clearly on Frederick's side in political matters and agreed with him that there should be a separation of spiritual and secular leadership. I have read these two works of Dante's in preparation for this book, and I see how Frederick influenced one of the icons of the Western tradition.

What Frederick's relevance is to our current situation will be judged by anyone who learns about his life. My own feeling is that he is one of those very interesting persons who was the center of attention during his lifetime. He had many staunch friends and colleagues who thought very highly of him, to the extent of giving him the title by which he is still referred to today, *Stupor Mundi*, or "Wonder of the World." He had just as many enemies, who called him every insult. As most of these enemies were churchmen at a time when the Roman Catholic Church had a near monopoly on education, the most effective propaganda against Frederick is literate and extreme. "Antichrist" was probably the strongest religious epithet that could be used during those times, and Frederick was called that for a long period of his life.

Both points of view can be justified, though probably not to the degrees they were held. Frederick was a great state builder. During his life, the Kingdom of Sicily, which included most of the peninsula of Italy south of Rome as well as the island, had the best administration of any state in Europe. He was much more tolerant of other religions than any other person in power during this time. He used methods and knowledge from other cultures, which was unusual in that rather insular time. The use of observation in gaining scientific knowledge was also quite unusual. He stated this clearly in the introduction to his falconry book: "Our intention is to set forth the things which are, as they are."[1]

His enemies had lots of ammunition as well. While Frederick always considered himself a Roman Catholic Christian, he certainly did not fit the mold as the church saw it in the thirteenth century. He acted like other rulers of the day in his personal life, having eleven children out of wedlock. He felt that he was a superior being as the descendant of two royal houses, and that any actions he took to implement his world empire were justified. German historians are not too kind to him, as he gave away rights to princely states in Germany that slowed formation of a nation-state there during the time that England, France, Spain, and Portugal were becoming more coherent national states. He also fit his times in his cruelty to subjects who disobeyed or betrayed him.

It is my hope that this small effort will introduce readers to an extraordinary personality of the past whose sensibilities still resonate today.

1. T.C. Van Cleve, *The Emperor Frederick II of Hohenstaufen* (Oxford, 1972), 315.

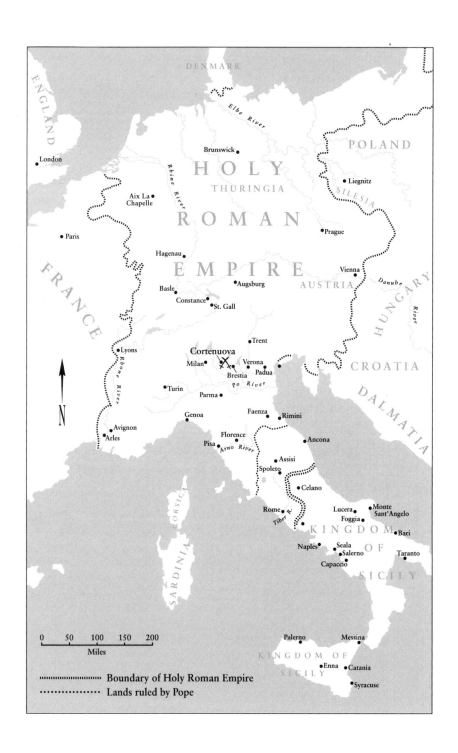

DENMARK

ENGLAND

London

Brunswick

HOLY

POLAND

Elbe River

Rhine River

THURINGIA

Liegnitz

SILESIA

Aix La
Chapelle

ROMAN

Paris

Prague

Hagenau

EMPIRE

Vienna

AUSTRIA

Danube River

HUNGARY

Basle

Augsburg

Constance

St. Gall

FRANCE

Trent

Lyons

Cortenuova

Milan

Verona

Padua

CROATIA

Brestia

Po River

Rhone River

Turin

Parma

DALMATIA

Genoa

Faenza

Rimini

Avignon

Florence

Arles

Pisa

Arno River

Ancona

Assisi

Spoleto

CORSICA

Celano

N

Rome

Tiber R.

Lucera

Monte
Sant'Angelo

Foggia

SARDINIA

KINGDOM

Bari

Naples

Seala

OF

Salerno

Taranto

Capaccio

SICILY

0   50   100 150 200
Miles

Palerno

Messina

KINGDOM OF

Enna

Catania

SICILY

Syracuse

•••••••••••••••••••• Boundary of Holy Roman Empire
•••••••••••• Lands ruled by Pope

ONE

Background and Antecedents

FREDERICK II WAS BORN TO RULE. He was the son of Henry VI, emperor of the Holy Roman Empire, and Constance of Sicily, heiress to the Kingdom of Sicily. At this time, the empire covered a vast portion of western Europe, from Campagna in Italy to Holstein in Denmark, from Burgundy in France to Pomerania in northeastern Germany. In the Europe of his time, only the holdings of the English king compared in size and wealth to either of these realms. Frederick eventually became ruler of the empire and the Kingdom of Sicily, the most powerful sovereign in Europe during the first half of the thirteenth century.

The Holy Roman emperors were considered the western successors to the Roman emperors, even though the only direct, unbroken Roman rule was that of the Byzantine emperors of the east, which continued until 1204. The declaration of Charlemagne as emperor in 800 started the history of the Holy

Roman Empire, and it was still a vital institution in the twelfth century. The Holy Roman emperors were considered the successors to the idea of a world empire that the Roman Empire embodied.

THE HOHENSTAUFEN SIDE

One of the scientific ideas of Frederick's time was that the main influence on the character of an individual came from the father. It was believed that the male contribution to a child was the active ingredient, and the female was a passive receptor in this process (as stated by Dante in canto 25 of the *Purgatorio*). From the way he treated women during his life, it appears that Frederick believed this as well. Hence, Frederick would have considered the influence of his paternal line extremely important in the formation of his character. This was true even though he did not know any of these ancestors, because his father died when he was two. He had the ideas they represented, uncontaminated by opinions of the people involved. Hence, the first subject to take up is these ancestors.

Frederick's grandfather and namesake was the Holy Roman Emperor Frederick I Barbarossa (Italian for "red beard"). Barbarossa was born circa 1123, the first son of Duke Frederick II, the second duke of Swabia in southwest Germany, and his wife, Judith. This was during a time of conflict between the Hohenstaufen and the Welfs, the leading noble families in the empire, who had contended for the office of emperor during the prior decades. Many leaders of the empire felt that Barbarossa, because of his parentage, could end this conflict. His father was a Hohenstaufen, and his mother was the daughter of Henry IX, duke of Bavaria and leader of the Welfs.

Barbarossa was elected German king on March 4, 1152, in Frankfurt. He succeeded his uncle, Conrad III. At the death in

1125 of the first Hohenstaufen emper-
or, Henry V, the electors of the empire
rejected the hereditary principle. They
selected Lothair of Saxony as emperor
over Conrad, who was the nephew of
Henry V. Conrad rebelled and was
elected king in Nuremburg in 1127 by
German opponents of Lothair's, and
king of Italy in June 1128. He raised an
army and fought against Lothair until
1135, when he submitted, was par-
doned, and recovered his estates in
Germany. After Lothair died in 1137,
Conrad was elected emperor in the
presence of the papal representative, or
legate, and crowned in Aachen in

Holy Roman Emperor
Frederick I, "Barbarossa,"
the Hohenstaufen grandfa-
ther of Frederick II.
(*Vatican Library*)

March 1138. He was never crowned in Rome as emperor. His
only son, Henry, died before him, so he designated Barbarossa
as his successor. The electors honored his request after he died
in 1152.

Like most of the people elected German king, Barbarossa
styled himself as emperor immediately after his election in
Germany. This was common, even though the pope always contended that a person elected German king did not become Holy
Roman emperor until crowned by the pope. The only people
who were elected German king and did not style themselves
emperor were minors, whose fathers were emperor, and were
elected German king as an indication that they would succeed
their fathers. Even then, the electors could choose not to honor
the emperor's request after he died. There were also times when
the election was disputed, and two people, each chosen by a
faction of the electors, styled themselves as emperor.

Barbarossa was confronted with a situation that had changed from the time of his predecessors. As a result of a long-standing dispute between the pope and the emperor, and the settlement of the Concordat of Worms, appointment of clerical posts in the empire resided with the pope. Early in his reign, Barbarossa ignored this, filling several vacant episcopal sees.

The preeminence of the empire was being challenged by the Byzantine Empire and by the newly powerful Kingdom of Sicily. Previous emperors had been able to keep the Lombard cities in northern Italy in line, but this problem turned out to be a major concern of Barbarossa's reign.

Even though Barbarossa was fighting with Pope Eugenius III over clerical appointments in Germany, he valued getting the crown of the Holy Roman Empire from him, so he set about to help him. The pope had problems with the commune, or local government, of Rome, which was led by Arnold of Brescia, and with the Kingdom of Sicily. Arnold was leading a revolt against the government of the pope. Barbarossa went to Rome and, with the pope's consent, arrested and hanged Arnold, solving that problem. The issue of Sicily was not resolved to Barbarossa's satisfaction, however, as its Norman rulers remained in place and, in 1156, received papal sanction for their rule in the Concordat of Benevento. Nevertheless, for his help, Barbarossa was crowned Holy Roman emperor by Pope Adrian IV in Rome on June 18, 1155.

The major problem all emperors faced was their relationship with the pope. The dispute over clerical appointments in the empire had supposedly passed, but it really continued all the way through the reign of Frederick II. In 1157, Barbarossa received a letter from Eugenius's successor, Pope Adrian IV, who casually mentioned that the empire was a *beneficium*, bestowed by the pope. This Latin term could mean "benefit," implying no subordination of emperor to pope. It could also be interpreted in a feudal sense, a property granted by the pope to his vassal. Barbarossa made clear to Adrian that he held his crowns from God alone, once he was elected by the German princes. This contentious relationship mostly played out in Italy.

Barbarossa had the problem all emperors had, that of ruling a large empire. The main division was between German-speaking areas and Italian-speaking areas. Neither had any political cohesion at the time, except that supplied by the empire. Most emperors had to treat these areas quite differently.

Barbarossa was the feudal leader of the empire. In the areas north of Italy, this meant granting fiefs and determining who would be the rulers. The second most important ruler in the empire was Duke Henry the Lion, ruler of Saxony. Barbarossa bestowed the duchies of Mecklenburg and Bavaria on him, and granted him the right to invest bishops in the area east of the Elbe, which was newly settled by German speakers. Henry then founded the towns of Lubeck and Munich, and brought German merchants to the Baltic. In 1158, Barbarossa elevated Duke Vladislav II of Bohemia to king, and also made Waldemar I of Denmark a vassal with rights that allowed Waldemar to proclaim the Kingdom of Denmark.

At this time, German settlers were moving east into Brandenburg (the area where Berlin is now) under Albert I (the Bear), who became margrave of Brandenburg. They were also moving east into Silesia (the area south of Brandenburg and north of the current Czech Republic). Barbarossa led expeditions into Poland in 1157 and 1172, and renewed the feudal ties of the Polish dukes, who were concerned with the German settlers moving into their area. These areas were near the areas ruled by Henry the Lion, and Henry tried to become more influential there. Henry engaged in feuds with several of his neighboring rulers, including Archbishop Wichmann of Magdeburg, Albert the Bear of Brandenburg, Louis III of Thuringia, and Archbishop Rainald of Cologne. These feuds irritated Barbarossa, and, along with Henry's refusal to help Barbarossa deal with the Lombard communes in Italy in 1176, led to Henry's deposition in 1180. The deposition was orchestrated by Barbarossa but accomplished by a council of princes in Geinhausen. Henry lost his dukedom and fled to England with his wife, Mathilde of England, a daughter of Henry II and Eleanor of Aquitaine. Barbarossa awarded the territories Henry the Lion had ruled to various dukes and archbishops. The awarding of Bavaria to Otto of Wittelsbach initiated a dynasty that ruled Bavaria until 1918.

This collective action led to the strengthening of the feudal system as a basis of the imperial constitution. There was no written constitution as we understand it. The custom of an emperor being the overlord, granting fiefs and adjudicating disputes, is what held the empire together. Only those who received their realms directly from the emperor became imperial princes. Barbarossa elevated several dukes to princes and used archbishops in the area as rulers as well. This led to increasing power for these princes and a continuing decentralization of power in the empire.

Barbarossa solved this problem of decreasing imperial power in one area of the empire by direct, personal action. In Burgundy in 1152, he appointed Duke Berthold IV of Zahringen as his personal representative, and in 1156, Barbarossa married Beatrix, the daughter of Count Rainald of Burgundy. This section of the empire gave Barbarossa very little trouble during his reign.

The other part of the empire that gave him few problems was the imperial territory, which consisted of his personal possessions, such as Swabia and various other landholdings. These included castles, cities, and ministerial seats that stretched from Swabia to Thuringia in central Germany. Barbarossa ruled these directly through imperial ministeriales, or ministers, who were mostly members of his personal circle.

During Barbarossa's reign, there were always struggles in the north, but no full-scale wars that required major military effort. The north was mainly a source of knights and other military resources to be used in the south, for the main struggles that consumed Barbarossa took place in Italy.

Barbarossa was determined to rule in the Italian-speaking parts of the empire, which consisted of what is today Italy north of Tuscany. The rule of the empire in northern Italy had become much less direct in the previous century. This was one of the most urbanized areas of Europe, and many towns there had been granted limited self-government, or commune status, by prior emperors. In the absence of permanent imperial forces, the stronger towns attempted to take over smaller neighboring towns. Barbarossa first heard of this at the Diet of Constance in 1153, when two dispossessed citizens of Lodi complained of the conquest of their town by Milan. Milan was the most powerful of the Lombard communes and had taken advantage of the absence of imperial authority in the prior decades to build a large territory between the north Italian lakes and the Apennine Mountains. Barbarossa felt that he had the right to render judgment, as emperor, on actions such as this conquest by Milan. He felt that reimposition of imperial rights would lead to peace; instead it led to war.

Barbarossa did not really understand the communes. In theory, there was equality among all citizens, and this was to lead to municipal government. Realistically, the aristocratic factions, the large rural landholders, and the prosperous merchants ran these communes for their own benefit. Enclaves controlled by the leading families remained in the towns, even though the municipal government of the towns worked hard to eliminate them. These conditions led to turbulence that struck the Hohenstaufen emperors as acute disorder subject to the correction of a supreme judge: the emperor. Distressed parties appealed to the emperor in many instances. This situation was the source of the image we have of Renaissance Italian towns as hotbeds of rivalry. It was also the beginning of the split into the Guelf (antiemperor) and Ghibelline (proemperor) factions. These names did not come into common use until the next century, but the conditions were already in place.

Barbarossa proved he meant business by marching into Lombardy in 1158, conquering, sacking, and eventually razing Milan. He convened a meeting of the commune leaders at Roncaglia to define and guarantee the rights of the emperor. Because the towns were prosperous, Barbarossa believed that, as overlord, he was entitled to approximately thirty thousand pounds of silver annually. He also believed that imperial officials should control the area, rather than the towns being allowed to exercise any self-government. The citizens of Milan rebuilt their walls and eventually repopulated the city, and the communes of Lombardy eventually felt that the emperor posed more of a threat than their expansionist neighbors. This led to the creation of the Lombard League in 1167; its explicit purpose was to resist the demands of the emperor. Barbarossa was surprised that the towns were able to ally themselves in any way, but the Lombard League became a fact in the politics of the Holy Roman Empire. The league grew more powerful after it became allied with the papacy soon after its formation in 1167.

Barbarossa had inherited a struggle between emperors and popes that had been going on for several centuries. In 1159, the pope that had crowned Barbarossa emperor, Adrian IV, died. The subsequent papal election resulted in a split decision, leading to a schism. Pope Alexander III was elected by a majority of cardinals and was immediately recognized by the Sicilian king. Another faction of cardinals elected Pope Victor IV, who was eventually recognized by Barbarossa. Barbarossa accompanied Victor to Rome in 1162 and displaced Alexander in the Vatican. Alexander III excommunicated Barbarossa in 1160, and gathered the support of the kings of France, England, Hungary, and Spain, and of Emperor Manuel of Byzantium. Alexander retired to France in 1162, where he remained until Barbarossa left Italy in 1165.

Alexander and Barbarossa continually negotiated to end the schism, but no agreements were reached. When Victor IV died in 1164, a new opposing pope was elected, Paschal III. This was done without Barbarossa's approval, so he sought other ways to deal with Alexander. This led to negotiations with Henry II of England, who was having problems with Alexander regarding the dispute between Henry and Archbishop of Canterbury Thomas Becket about the jurisdiction of state courts over crimes of the clergy. Barbarossa promised Henry that he would not recognize Alexander while Henry kept the pressure on Alexander to settle the Becket problem.

After the death of William I of Sicily in 1166, Barbarossa decided that another expedition to Italy was necessary to deal with the Lombard cities and with the pope. He had gone to Italy in 1153, which eventually led to his crowning by Pope Adrian IV, and in 1158 he had returned to deal with Milan and the Lombard cities. In 1162, he had campaigned in the Papal States, which consisted of the provinces of Romagna, Ancona, Spoleto, Sabina, and Campagna, and the Patrimony of St. Peter in central Italy. The Patrimony of St. Peter consisted of the portion of the Papal States west of the Tiber, and included Rome. During the 1162 campaign, Barbarossa had considered invading the Kingdom of Sicily. His expedition in 1167 concentrated the minds of the Lombard cities enough to finalize their formation of the Lombard League. But once again his action turned out to be futile, this time because of an outbreak of malaria in his army. Barbarossa had led mostly German armies into Italy before, and the problem of disease had always been present.

In 1174, after Barbarossa had helped make peace between Henry II of England and Louis VII of France and started negotiations with the Byzantine Empire, he launched yet another campaign in Italy, intending to deal with the Lombard cities militarily. He was able to keep an army there for two years, but he had counted on Henry the Lion to lead more troops from Germany to Italy. Henry refused to come to his aid, and the Lombard League defeated Barbarossa at Legnano. The defeat of Barbarossa's army of about ten thousand by a similar force of Lombards stymied any more offensive action by the emperor and led to negotiations with Alexander III. Barbarossa and the pope signed a treaty at Anagni in 1176 that secured the end of Barbarossa's excommunication. The next year in Venice, Barbarossa formally recognized Alexander as the true pope and received the kiss of peace from Alexander in the town square. Barbarossa continued to put military and legal pressure on the Lombard League, finally resulting in the Treaty of Constance in 1183 that ended the military conflict.

The net result of all this was a reduction of imperial power in northern Italy. Barbarossa had to recognize that the Lombard towns could collect their own tolls and taxes, and he granted this right in perpetuity. He still attempted to control the consular elections in northern Italian towns but did not have much success in those that were members of the Lombard

League. He tried, with some success, to wear down the unity of the league.

But he was more successful in the newly acquired territories of Tuscany and the neighboring Apennines. He had received these lands from the will of the Saxon Duke Welf VI. They were known as the Matildine legacy. The original holder, Countess Matilda, had good relations with the papacy in the eleventh century, and the Vatican still considered itself protector of this legacy. Barbarossa was able to secure acceptance of his rule in Tuscany and Umbria by his lighter touch in administration after the 1177 Venice agreement with Alexander. Hence, during the last years of Barbarossa's reign, there was a period of peace between the emperor and the Lombard cities.

Barbarossa's son, Henry, was born in 1165. He was chosen German king, at Barbarossa's urging, in 1169, and was crowned at Aachen in August. Barbarossa negotiated the marriage of Henry to Constance of Sicily, and they were wed in Milan in January 1186. With succession in place, Barbarossa felt free to return to crusading.

Barbarossa had accompanied Emperor Conrad III, his uncle, on the Second Crusade, in 1147. It had not been a happy experience, as Conrad's army was defeated by the Turks at Dorylaeum in southern Anatolia. The army was mostly destroyed, and with the survivors, Conrad retreated to Nicea in northern Anatolia. He was able to join Louis VII of France in the Holy Land the next year. An attack on Damascus followed, and it failed. Conrad and his nephew returned to Constantinople and then to the Holy Roman Empire.

By the time of the Third Crusade, in 1189, Barbarossa was in his late sixties. He had settled his differences with the papacy and responded positively to the appeal of Pope Gregory VIII to go on crusade, feeling that his son could rule the empire in his absence. He gathered the most formidable crusader army yet, consisting of more than six thousand German knights and foot soldiers. This army marched via the pilgrim route through the Balkans and Byzantine Empire. The army had almost reached its objective when, while crossing the Saleph River in southern Anatolia, Barbarossa drowned on June 10, 1190. He was about sixty-seven years old, and had been Holy Roman emperor thirty-eight years.

After taking the reins from his father in 1189, Henry spent the next year or so putting down a rebellion by Henry the Lion in Saxony. A settlement was reached, and Henry of Hohenstaufen was able to proceed to Italy, where he was crowned Holy Roman Emperor Henry VI by Pope Celestine III in April 1191. One result of this trip to Italy was that Henry the Lion resumed his rebellion in 1191. Henry VI was forced to return to Germany.

On his return, Henry VI had two major concerns. Richard the Lion-Hearted of England had been captured on his way back from the Holy Land by Henry VI's vassal Leopold, Duke of Austria, in December 1192. Leopold and Richard had been on crusade together and became enemies while in the Holy Land. Leopold turned Richard over to Henry VI in February 1193, and Henry conducted negotiations with Richard's mother, Eleanor of Aquitaine. This resulted in Richard agreeing to surrender his kingdom to the empire, receive it back as a fief, and pay a ransom of one hundred fifty thousand marks (approximately fifteen million dollars today). Henry VI was continuing the idea of a world empire with the Holy Roman emperor as the successor to the Roman emperor.

Henry VI's other concern was the continuing rebellion of Henry the Lion. This occupied Henry VI until March 1194, when a treaty was signed with Henry the Lion confirming

Henry VI as emperor and overlord. Henry VI then turned his attention to Italy and the Sicilian kingdom. His actions there will be covered in the next chapter.

After the birth of his son, Frederick, in December 1194, Henry VI wanted to secure Frederick's succession. This led to several conferences with the princes of the empire, who refused to make succession to the throne hereditary. However, Henry VI was able to get Frederick elected German king in December 1196. Henry VI died of malaria in Messina, Sicily, on September 28, 1197.

The German side of Frederick's inheritance gave him a strong claim to the crown of the Holy Roman Empire. Frederick was born in Italy, and raised in the Kingdom of Sicily. We now turn to that inheritance.

THE HAUTEVILLE LINE

Someone living in the thirteenth century would have believed that his father's inheritance was more important than his mother's, but Frederick's forebears on his mother's side are certainly as interesting as those on his father's side, and her legacy was equally important.

Frederick's maternal grandfather was King Roger II of Sicily. He was a descendant and product of the Norman expansion that took place in the eleventh century. The two main results of this expansion from Normandy were the conquest of England by William the Conqueror and the eventual formation of the Kingdom of Sicily. William ruled Normandy as well as England, of which he became king. The formation of the Kingdom of Sicily happened in a more random manner.

At the beginning of the eleventh century, Sicily and southern Italy were a hodgepodge of competing Latin, Lombard, Greek, and Arab principalities. The various rulers were always looking for military help in their disputes with neighboring rulers. This led to the use of the leading mercenaries of the time, Norman knights, the best fighters in Europe. In the early eleventh century, Norman mercenaries started to come to this area in greater numbers, equipped for war. Eventually they started acquiring their own estates, mostly in southern Italy. The leading group to emerge from this stew was led by the sons of Tancred of Hauteville. The largest remaining realms in the area fell late in the eleventh century to the sons of Tancred, Robert Guiscard and Roger. Byzantines were finally expelled from Bari in 1071, and Palermo, home of the most powerful Arab emirate, was conquered in 1072. Guiscard took the lead in dealing with the papacy and in conquering the areas of southwest Italy. Roger handled the toe of Italy, and together they acquired the island of Sicily, finishing their actions there with the taking of Messina in 1091.

The Holy Roman Empire still had claims to this part of Italy, even though it had been over a century since any emperor had come south of Rome. So Guiscard and Roger protected themselves from the emperor by helping the papacy.

The papacy was also interested in the religious makeup of southern Italy and Sicily. It was an irritant to the popes that, at a time when the church was successfully converting the people of northern and eastern Europe, these areas close to Rome were mostly non-Roman Catholic. Apulia and Calabria had large Greek populations, and their churches were subservient to the Greek Orthodox Church. At least half the population of Sicily was Muslim. The popes approved of the Hauteville action to conquer these territories and expected the result to be a Roman Catholic domain.

By the later eleventh century, Guiscard's interest had turned to Byzantine lands in Greece and the Holy Land. This left

Roger to rule Sicily and southwestern Italy. In 1098, Pope Urban II, the originator of the First Crusade, awarded Roger status equivalent to an apostolic legate in his territories. That gave Roger authority to set up bishoprics, name bishops, and administer the church in his territories. At this same time, Guiscard's son Bohemond participated in the First Crusade and ended up as prince of Antioch. So the Hauteville family was serving the interests of the church and its own interests.

King Roger II of Sicily, the Hauteville grandfather of Frederick II, and first king of the Kingdom of Sicily. (*Liber ad honorem Augusti*)

The grant of power to Roger by the pope made sense, as these territories were being conquered by Catholic lords for the first time since the sixth century, and the church infrastructure needed to be set up. Roger and his successors took this up with enthusiasm.

Roger's title at his death was count of Sicily and Calabria, vassal of the duke of Apulia, who was a vassal of the pope's. Roger died in 1101, leaving two young sons, Simon and Roger, and his wife, Adelaide of Savona, as regent. Simon was expected to succeed to the title on attaining his majority, but he died in 1105. Roger the son spent the years before his majority in Sicily and Calabria. He was knighted in Palermo in 1112, and declared Duke Roger II in his own right.

Roger II took over the rule of Sicily and Calabria. Other Norman lords ruled several areas south of Rome, and Roger was determined to bring them all under his control. He succeeded in becoming overlord of all southern Italy except Apulia by 1122. In 1127, his cousin Duke William of Apulia, his theoretical overlord, died without issue. Roger II claimed the inheritance. By this time, Roger was an experienced ruler, and he overcame the opposition of the Apulian nobility through force and diplomacy. Roger II was invested as duke of Sicily, Calabria, and Apulia by Pope Honorius II in 1128.

As a result of these events, Roger II was one of the most powerful lords in Europe. He controlled prosperous areas, and he maintained that control by retaining the Byzantine and Arab governmental institutions that were in place. This allowed for more central control than the feudal system in other parts of Europe. Roger felt that he deserved a kingdom, and a disputed papal election got him one.

In 1130, the death of Pope Honorius II led to the elections of Innocent II, who had the support of most of Europe, and Analectus II, who had Roger's support. Roger's price for this support was coronation as king of Sicily, which took place in Palermo on Christmas 1130. After the death of Analectus II in 1138, Roger II defeated a papal army and captured Innocent II, who was forced to confirm Roger II as king of Sicily and over-lord of Italy south of the Garigliano River. Roger II used this status to put down any remaining insurrections on the main-land, which had been abetted by Pope Innocent and by the emperor. He had always kept strong control in Sicily, so after an effective rule of twenty-six years, he achieved the internal peace he wanted in his realms.

Roger's father had essentially been a Norman knight, ruling his realm as such. Roger II, however, was born in Sicily and raised there. Hence he had a more Mediterranean background, and that is reflected in his actions and interests. The government he headed operated in three languages—Latin, Greek, and Arabic—and he was influenced by many different cultures. He adopted some western feudal practices and institutions, such as the parliament of his barons who met in Melfi in 1129 and subsequently approved his acts as lawmaker and king. He followed Byzantine practices, particularly after he became king. Most of the decrees he issued that survive were in Greek. He held himself out to his Muslim subjects as protector, though not one, of the faithful. Because his subjects were more diverse than those in other European realms, he used all the raw material he found to try to mold a workable system.

Roger II considered himself a good Roman Catholic and had good relations with the papacy. He was the main administrator of the church in his territories, based on his understanding of the agreement his father signed with Pope Urban II. During Roger II's reign, it appears that the percentage of Catholics in his territories rose, mainly by immigration of Catholics from northern Italy and Europe. The percentages of the Greek Orthodox and Muslim populations decreased. There was no persecution of these religions during his reign, but the higher-ranking Muslims serving at court were expected to convert. Some Muslim leaders argued that the faithful had a religious obligation to leave Christian rule. It appears this teaching had some effect.

Roger also found the justification for his autonomous rule in the Rome of Constantine and Justinian. He held himself out to the Byzantine emperor in 1143 as a *basileus*, equal to the emperor. The Byzantines were outraged to the point of imprisoning the ambassador bearing this message. However, Roger was able to act as an emperor in his kingdom. He had better administration than other states in his area, and hence collected more taxes and other income. He had inherited the navy his father built, and that gave him more autonomy. He had accepted his realm from the pope but was not dependent on the papacy. Roger II was able to act as an independent force in the Mediterranean.

As a result, he expanded his power in several directions. Roger II was irritated by North African piracy, a problem that continued until the nineteenth century. His solution was to create a small North African province around Tripoli. He based some of his navy there, which limited the reach of the pirates. Sicilian rule lasted until after Roger's death, when the province was conquered by the new Islamic power, the Almohads from the Morocco area.

Roger II also had interests in the crusader states—small Christian states ruled by noble crusaders and their descendents that had been established in the Holy Land after the First Crusade, and in Spain—which he explored diplomatically. He was continually dealing with the Byzantine and Holy Roman emperors, and he had minor conflicts with both. He corresponded with the rulers of Egypt, an unusual act for a Catholic ruler, and made a trade agreement with them. While his power did not extend much beyond Sicily and southern Italy, Roger II was a major player in the politics of the Mediterranean.

The basis for this was his practical, effective administration of his realm. The main crop was durum wheat, which was easily transported and did not spoil. Hence it could be shipped all over the area. This trade was controlled by the crown in Sicily, and in royal lands in southern Italy. Sicily's location on the main trade routes of the Mediterranean also led to significant income. The regalian, or ruler's, rights to resources such as salt, iron, and tuna fish were exercised to generate more income. Administration of justice in the realm created fees and hence was profitable to the monarchy. Roger II was also adept at securing income from foreign affairs, such as payments from the Byzantine emperor following naval actions against his possessions in Greece and Asia Minor. It was felt at the time that the Kingdom of Sicily was the richest realm in Europe, aside from Byzantium, which was mostly an Asian power. Roger II appears to have been an efficient manager of administrators who operated on the basis of Latin, Greek, and Arabic methods, and a good manager of money, leaving a full treasury for his successors.

His wealth allowed Roger II to keep a lavish court for his time. Silk cloth was manufactured there and used for royal regalia. There were lavish entertainments, and subsidies for many intellectual projects. Several large buildings were erected during this time, including palaces and churches. These buildings reflect the various cultures that surrounded them. The cathedral at Cefelu, on the mainland, shows little Arabic influence. The Palatine Chapel in Palermo shows Latin, Byzantine, and Arabic features, as does the Church of San Giovanni degli Eremiti.

Roger's main interest outside governing was science. He sponsored the translation of many books that had been received from Constantinople. These included Ptolemy's *Almagest*, works by Plato, and sibylline oracles. The other main center of translation at this time was Toledo, Spain. At Toledo, the translations were done from several languages, including Greek, Syriac, Arabic, and Latin. In Sicily, most of the work was done directly from Greek to Latin. In Spain, translations were done in greater numbers. At the same time, Arabs and Jews completed commentaries on the translations, which eased their acceptance into western Europe. Both Toledo and Sicily were prized as points of access to the learning of ancient Greece and Rome.

Roger II sponsored one writer whose work became known at the time and continues to interest scholars. This was al-Idrisi, an Arabic political refugee from North Africa. His area of expertise was geography, which also interested Roger. Al-Idrisi created a well-known silver map of the world for Roger, which was kept in Palermo until it was destroyed in a sacking of the palace in 1161. He also wrote the *Kitab Rujar*, or *Book of Roger*, which shows the real working of a multicultural court.

The range of knowledge was impressive in the parts of the world that al-Idrisi was familiar with and that his fellow Arabs had traveled in (Sicily, southern Italy, Spain, North Africa). When describing India and China, he indulged in fantasy, as did most other geographies of the time. What were surprising were his descriptions of Northern and western Europe. Roger's court was filled with people from those areas. Al-Idrisi seems to have had no regard for works of Latin geographers and did not regard eyewitness accounts of Latins the same as he did Arabs. The various cultures at court existed beside each other but did not necessarily instruct each other.

Roger II was married three times. He outlived his first two wives, and by the time he died in 1154, he had one remaining son, William, to carry on the rule. He also left his final wife, married in his last year of life, pregnant with what turned out to be Constance of Sicily. Roger's son William I ruled from 1154 to 1166. He was nicknamed the Bad by his enemies and charged with spending all his time in the harem and pleasure palace in Palermo. Considering all he accomplished, though, he must have gotten out a bit. He dealt with a Byzantine invasion of Apulia in 1155, eventually expelling them after a victory at Brindisi. And there were continual rebellions by various barons, leading to the sacking of the Palermo palace in 1161. Eventually he was able to regain control of the realm, which he passed intact (except for the North African province lost to the Almohads) to his son in 1166.

William I was succeeded by his son, William II, who was twelve when his father died, so a regency headed by his mother ruled until 1171. Upon taking power, William II kept the peace with the barons and towns of his realm. This led to his being nicknamed the Good, in contrast to his father. The leading barons and towns of the Kingdom of Sicily remembered his reign as their golden age, especially after Frederick II took control of the kingdom. William II's main interest was foreign affairs, particularly dealing with the pope and with the Byzantine and Holy Roman emperors.

William II approached Byzantine Emperor Manuel I and attempted to form a marriage alliance with his daughter, Maria. Manuel rejected the idea, which turned William against the Byzantines. He concluded a truce with Barbarossa, which was part of the Venice settlement in 1177. But William II had been restrained by Pope Alexander III from taking revenge on the Byzantine Empire.

After the death of Alexander III, he decided to act against Byzantium. To protect his northern frontier, he negotiated the marriage of his Aunt Constance of Sicily to Barbarossa's heir, Henry. The marriage took place in Milan in 1186. William II then attacked the Byzantines in Macedonia and Thrace, and was on the verge of attacking Constantinople before he was defeated by the Byzantine navy. He had previously been unsuccessful in reestablishing Roger II's North African possessions. William II was intending to go on the Third Crusade when he died in 1189.

William II was childless, so the family claim to the Kingdom of Sicily passed to his Aunt Constance, who was married to Henry of Hohenstaufen. Constance was ten years older than Henry and had not had any children by the time William II died. This did not keep Henry from claiming the Sicilian crown in his wife's name. This was a change from Barbarossa's claim that the Kingdom of Sicily was a bandit kingdom, subject to conquest by its overlord, the Holy Roman emperor. Henry intended to maintain the separation of the kingdom from the empire. The kingdom was not subject to elections by German princes, and it was to be held as a private possession of the Hohenstaufens'.

The south Italian nobles did not agree. In 1190, they convened a parliament and elected a bastard son of Constance's dead brother Roger, Tancred, Count of Lecce, as king. Tancred knew that Henry would be down in his area sometime soon, so he tried to ingratiate himself with the barons and towns of southern Italy, gathering support for the inevitable conflict. Henry made an effort to deal with Tancred during his trip to Rome to be crowned emperor, but disease in the German army stationed near Naples, as well as continuing problems with Henry the Lion, required the newly crowned emperor Henry VI to return to Germany.

Henry VI's next expedition south led to success. He made peace with the Lombard towns in January 1194, ensuring their loyalty for awhile. Tancred died in February 1194, leaving only a young son as heir. Henry's appearance in southern Italy in May 1194 met little resistance, and the final result was that he entered Palermo in November 1194 and was crowned king of Sicily, duke of Apulia and the principality of Capua on Christmas 1194. The next day the life began that is the inspiration for this book.

TWO

Early Years

H ENRY'S WIFE, CONSTANCE, was traveling in December 1194 to join her husband in the Sicilian domain he claimed in her name. She had been married since 1186, and was now forty years old. She was also pregnant for the first time. During the trip, it became clear that the child would be born before she reached her husband in Sicily. Constance stopped in the town of Jesi, in the March of Ancona, a province on the east-central coast of Italy. The sources agree that the birth of a son took place in Jesi on December 26, 1194. Some sources state this event took place in a tent in the square of Jesi, open to witnesses, to confirm that the child was born of Constance, who was well past the normal age of childbearing. Due to Constance's age, a legend grew up that Frederick was really the son of a butcher of Jesi, substituted on this date, as Constance could not be having her first child so late in life.

Constance was born after the death of her father, Roger II of Sicily. Not much is known about her life until her marriage. She lived in the Kingdom of Sicily and seems to have become very fond of the island. Several chronicles state that she had been in a convent before her nephew, William II, married her off to the heir of the Hohenstaufen, Henry VI. Dante was convinced enough to include her in the *Paradiso*, canto 3. She was used as an example of broken vows, leaving a convent in order to contract a political marriage. There is evidence that Constance was in a convent, but none that she had taken vows as a nun. It was common for aristocratic women to be raised in a convent after the death of a parent.

Constance originally named her son Constantine, after herself and the long-ago Roman Emperor Constantine the Great. Constance proceeded to Bari, where she met her husband and was crowned queen of the Kingdom of Sicily. The baby Constantine had been left with the duke of Spoleto. After a short time in Bari, Henry appointed Constance as head of a regency council for the Kingdom of Sicily, and he headed north to Germany. It is possible Henry stopped off on his way to see his son in Spoleto, but it is not verified that he ever did see him. The first stop on Henry's trip was Rome, where he sought to have his new son confirmed as king of the Romans, another title used by the electors of the emperor. If the person elected king of the Romans was an adult, he immediately styled himself as emperor. King of the Romans was also used as a title when the electors selected a minor, when the emperor was still alive. Henry accomplished his goal in Rome: his son was named king of the Romans before he was baptized. The baptism took place soon afterward, in Assisi, in the presence of fifteen cardinals and bishops, but neither parent. The baby's baptismal name was Frederick Roger, after both his grandfathers.

Henry's return to Germany led to the election of Frederick as German king in 1196. But then Henry needed to return to

Sicily. Constance was the focus of Sicilian discontent with Henry's cruel imposition of rule in 1194, and also because of Sicilian resentment of the Germans who had accompanied Henry and stayed. It is not known if Constance's presence directly inspired any revolts, but some did take place. Henry returned to Sicily and dealt decisively with the revolts and the rebels. His revenge was in line with the normal cruelty of the twelfth century. In one famous case, he felt that Count Giordano had aspired to usurp his rule. Hence, the count's punishment was to be put onto a

Birth of Frederick II, December 26, 1194. This tent was in the marketplace of Jesi, to prove that Constance was giving birth at the advanced age of 40. (*Attilios*)

red-hot throne, and a red-hot crown was nailed to his head. Henry also indulged his suspicions of Constance by having her confined to the Palace of Palermo.

Henry had been preparing to go on crusade, so he planned to have his brother, Philip of Swabia, go to Sicily, get Frederick, and take him back to Germany to be crowned king and to remain there until Henry was done with his crusade. Philip was on his way to Sicily when Henry died of malaria in Messina on September 28, 1197. This led to a wave of anti-German feeling in all of Italy. Philip had to flee back to Swabia. Constance, who became regent of the Kingdom of Sicily, kept Frederick in her household.

There was a major dispute over Henry's will, with Constance believing she had the authority as head of the regency council and mother of Frederick to rule. Early on she tried to expel the

German adventurers led by Markward of Anweiler and his Sicilian supporters. Markward had accompanied Henry south as seneschal, or steward, of the imperial household, and was a leader of the German knights who had stayed in the Kingdom of Sicily. Constance had papal support in her attempt to expel these knights.

Constance suffered a serious illness in early 1198, but rallied sufficiently to hold a joint coronation of Frederick and herself in Palermo in early summer of 1198. Soon, however, it became clear that her illness was mortal, and she determined to have Frederick made a ward of the pope. She put this in her will, secured papal agreement, and died November 27, 1198, in Palermo.

Frederick's guardian was to be the new pope, Innocent III. Born Lotario de Segni of a good Roman family, he was in his late 30s when raised to the papacy. Lotario had been trained as a theologian in Paris and a canon lawyer in Bologna. In 1190, Pope Clement III, possibly a relative of Lotario's, raised him to cardinal. Lotario's next years were spent in mostly intellectual pursuits, until he was unanimously elected pope on the day of the death of Celestine III, January 8, 1198.

When Innocent was negotiating with Constance over becoming Frederick's guardian, one of his conditions was that Constance take back the churchman Walter of Pelear as chancellor of the kingdom. Constance agreed, even though Walter had been in charge of her confinement in Palermo before Henry's death and was thought to be pro-German. Walter, bishop of Troia, was confirmed as chancellor and head of the regency council before Constance died. Upon her death, he became the dominant member of the council, taking immediate care and possession of Frederick in the name of the pope.

Even though Innocent III was Frederick's guardian, Innocent did not meet his ward until Frederick reached the age of majority, fourteen. His care was delegated to Walter. Walter seems to have been a Talleyrand-like figure who dealt with everyone, changed sides frequently, and survived. He ended up serving Frederick until the 1220s, when he left the kingdom before being charged by jealous associates with treason, and ended his days as a pensioner in Venice.

Walter appears to have kept Frederick with him from Constance's death in 1198 until autumn 1201. Then, during an invasion of the island of Sicily by Markward, Walter gave Frederick to his brother, Gentile, for safekeeping. Gentile took Frederick to the fortress of Castellamare in Palermo. During a siege of Palermo in autumn 1201, Gentile left the castle, reportedly to go to Messina to secure provisions. When Markward's forces took Palermo, Markward wanted the body of the anointed ruler of the kingdom, Frederick. He went to the castle, was let in by the castellan, or warden, and found the boy.

In a letter to the pope, Archbishop Rainald of Capua gave a contemporary report of the events that followed. It provides the first insight into the character of Frederick, who impressed the archbishop:

> When by the treachery of those who had care of him, they had penetrated into the inmost part of the palace and came forward to lay their hands upon him, and it was clear to him that he was now in the hands of his enemies, he, who had hardly emerged from the age when he had been rocked to sleep with lullabies, defended himself with tears and force. Nor did he forget his royal estate when, like a mouse who fears the pursuit of a ferocious animal, he threw himself upon those who

were about to seize him, trying with all his force to ward off the arm of him who dared to lay his hand upon the sacred body of the Lord's anointed; then rending his clothes from off him, filled with impotent rage, he tore at his soft flesh with his sharp nails.[1]

It seems remarkable today that someone who was less than seven years old and had been raised by guardians since age three would be so aware of his special status. Deepening the mystery of Frederick's upbringing is that he was handed over to an associate of Markward's, William Capparone. How Frederick spent the next seven years of his life is unknown. Georgina Masson and Ernst Kantorowicz posit a carefree existence on the streets of Palermo.[2] During these years, Palermo had a substantial Arab population, and Frederick appears to have learned to speak Arabic about this time. He also had a Latin tutor, William Franciscus, from 1201 through 1206. Later, Frederick would say, "Before I assumed the responsibilities of government [at fourteen], I sought after knowledge and breathed her balsamic perfumes."[3]

It is clear that during this time, Frederick's character was formed, because it was fairly consistent afterward. He had a healthy self-regard for his own royal, and then imperial, status. He could speak several languages. One source says he spoke five by the age of fourteen (Italian, Latin, Greek, Arabic, and French), and it is known he learned to speak German before going to claim the imperial throne. He was skilled in the exercise of arms, and by age fourteen was a fine horseman. He was

1. Georgina Masson, *Frederick II of Hohenstaufen* (New York, 1973), 31.

2. Ibid., 32; Ernst Kantorowicz, *Frederick the Second, 1194–1250*, trans. E.O. Lorimer (New York, 1957), 26–28.

3. Masson, *Frederick II of Hohenstaufen*, 32.

an omnivorous reader, and was keenly interested in nature and the study of the universe. It is also clear that he considered himself the Lord's anointed, and that his main mission in life was to rule. But the status of the territories he expected to rule was unclear at the time he reached the age of majority.

THE KINGDOM OF SICILY

Constance had been left as head of a regency council for the Kingdom of Sicily on the death of her husband. She could have claimed to be sole ruler as successor to her father, brother, and nephew, but does not appear to have done so. She made sure that she and her son were crowned at the same time in Palermo in the summer of 1198, and later she signed an agreement with the pope to make Frederick his ward upon her death. But other conditions of the agreement were not so favorable. Constance agreed to accept the crown as a vassal of the pope's. She also gave the pope rights to run the church in the kingdom, which the kings had done since the early twelfth century. These concessions made the regency council one of the power centers in the kingdom at the time of her death. But it was not the only power center.

When Henry VI went to Sicily in 1194 and 1197, he brought along many German knights to make up his fighting forces, and they helped him take control of the kingdom both times. Some of these knights intended to go on crusade with Henry, but that plan fell apart when he died. Henry had undoubtedly promised territorial rewards, and after his death, the German knights started taking them. They acted no differently than the Normans who had come along with the Hautevilles, or the French and Aragonese companions of subsequent conquerors of the kingdom. They wanted tangible rewards for long and dangerous service with a feudal lord.

As a result, there were two factions in the kingdom, one led by the regency council and an opposing faction of German knights. Constance had used her position to try to banish the German knights from the kingdom in early 1198. Markward of Anweiler, seneschal of the empire and imperial representative in the March of Ancona, led these knights. This faction ignored the banishment and waged a military campaign against the regency council. Markward had a power base in southern Italy and claimed to have the correct will of Henry VI, which showed Markward as regent, and he also claimed to be a loyal follower of Henry VI and Philip of Swabia.

After the death of Constance, Markward made a deal with the count of Malta, a Genoese privateer named Guglielmo Grasso, to supply ships for an invasion of Sicily. The invasion took place in November 1199, with Markward's forces landing at Trapani in western Sicily. The price of this support from Genoa was to let Genoa trade with Sicily with no customs dues, and free use of several ports on the island. The chancellor of Sicily, Walter of Pelear, was not sure how to respond to the invasion because he knew he did not have the military force to resist Markward. He kept Innocent III informed of events; the pope was already nervous about Markward and his power base in Ancona, about one hundred miles north of Rome.

Innocent responded to the invasion of Sicily with a letter to the Sicilian people dated November 24, 1199. The gist of this letter was that Markward, who had gotten help from Muslims in his invasion, was an oppressor of Christians and an ally of Muslims, and a worse infidel than a Muslim. The pope thought about declaring a crusade against Markward. He did not take that step, but he did secure military forces to defend Frederick's interest. The language used against Markward foreshadowed how later popes would deal with Frederick.

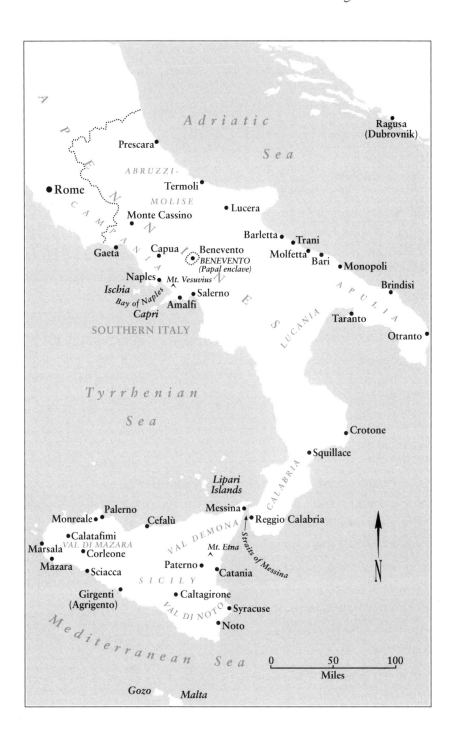

Ragusa
(Dubrovnik)

Adriatic

Sea

Prescara

ABRUZZI-

Termoli

Rome

MOLISE

Lucera

Monte Cassino

Barletta

Trani

Gaeta

Capua

Benevento

Molfetta

Bari

BENEVENTO
(Papal enclave)

Monopoli

Naples

Mt. Vesuvius

Brindisi

Ischia

Salerno

Bay of Naples

A P U L I A

Capri

Amalfi

L U C A N I A

Taranto

SOUTHERN ITALY

Otranto

Tyrrhenian

Sea

Crotone

Squillace

C A L A B R I A

Lipari
Islands

Palerno

Messina

Monreale

Cefalù

Reggio Calabria

Calatafimi

VAL DEMONA

VAL DI MAZARA

Mt. Etna

Straits of Messina

Marsala

Corleone

Mazara

Sciacca

Paterno

Catania

S I C I L Y

Girgenti
(Agrigento)

Caltagirone

VAL DI NOTO

Syracuse

Noto

M e d i t e r r a n e a n

S e a

0   50   100

Miles

N

Gozo   *Malta*

The leader of Innocent's force to contain Markward was a French knight, Walter of Brienne, who was the husband of King Tancred's daughter Alberia. Walter of Brienne had already taken crusader vows, but the pope convinced him to act against Markward instead. Walter of Brienne had to return to Champagne to recruit his army, which he did in the summer of 1201. By this time, Walter of Pelear had made a deal with Markward, left Sicily, and returned to his home area of southern Italy. One result of this was Markward's capture of Frederick in 1201.

Walter of Pelear supplied troops to a German army led by Markward's associate Dipold of Acerra, per his agreement with Markward. Walter of Brienne led a French army south, financed by the pope. He defeated the German followers of Markward's on the mainland near Capua, then continued to march south. He recovered the Duchy of Lecce, and the pope gave him the rule of Apulia and Campania. That satisfied him, and Walter of Brienne did not lead the papal army to Sicily to save Frederick.

Markward had suffered a defeat by other papal forces at Monreale outside Palermo in early 1201. This victory had not been followed up, and Markward's hold on Palermo and most of Sicily continued. Markward was in the process of besieging Messina when he died in late 1202. But this did not mean the end of the German party in the kingdom. William Capparone took Markward's place, occupying Palermo and taking possession of Frederick. He began calling himself Defender of the King and Great Captain of the Kingdom. William eventually agreed to acknowledge Innocent as his feudal lord. Innocent acquiesced to William's position in Sicily. Another German, Conrad von Urslingen, was granted authority by Philip of Swabia to rule in his name. But Philip really did not have any authority to give away. Walter of Brienne remained on the mainland until June 1205. While besieging a castle occupied by his old opponent Dipold of Acerra, Walter failed to place a guard on his own tent one night. Dipold and some companions came by, cut the ropes of the tent, captured Walter, and cut him to pieces.

Even though Pope Innocent III had grand ideas of papal supremacy based on the Donation of Constantine (a document supposedly from Emperor Constantine giving the popes authority over temporal rulers but subsequently proven to be fraudulent), he had little power in the Kingdom of Sicily until 1208. That year, a series of coups in Palermo passed power from William Capparone to Dipold of Acerra to Walter of Pelear. The physical possession of Frederick passed to a papal representative in Palermo. Pope Innocent had been obliged to deal with all the supposed rulers of Sicily. When he got control of Frederick, Innocent was confident enough to enter the kingdom in June 1208.

He subsequently called a council with the south Italian barons at San Germano, about one hundred miles southeast of Rome in the kingdom. Innocent's goal was to reconstruct the Norman administration of the kingdom on the mainland. He called on the barons to assist, and appointed justiciars and masters to adjudicate disputes. Even though Innocent did not wish to exercise direct control, he was restoring a system meant for exactly that. The officials were taken from the class of the great mainland barons. This continued the process that had been ongoing since the death of Henry VI, the dissipation of the powers and assets of the king.

At some point, Frederick decided to reverse this process. It is not clear how the pope determined that Frederick had reached his majority soon after his fourteenth birthday (his cousin King

William II did not ascend to the same throne until age seventeen, after a regency that lasted five years), but that was the decision. Innocent relinquished his guardianship but continued to be the feudal lord of Frederick for the Kingdom of Sicily. Frederick was granted authority as king of Sicily in early 1209.

THE HOLY ROMAN EMPIRE

The death of Frederick's father, Henry VI, in 1197, should have led to an election of a new emperor. Henry had tried to get the imperial electors to acknowledge the hereditary principle by having Frederick crowned while still a child, but the electors declined. They did elect Frederick German king in 1196, prior to Henry's death, but that was an honorary title due to Frederick's age. Henry had designated his brother, Philip of Swabia, to protect Frederick's interests in Germany. Henry had also given Philip charge of the Mathildine estates, consisting of Tuscany and adjacent parts of the Apennines. Because the pope felt he was protector of the Mathildine estates as well, it set up a conflict between Philip and the papacy. This became stronger after Philip was elected German king in March 1198. This election was disputed by some of the nobility of the empire, because they did not want another Hohenstaufen ruler. Another election later that year resulted in the selection of a son of Henry the Lion, Otto of Brunswick.

This situation led to a continuation of the dispute between the Hohenstaufen and Welf within the empire; Philip was from the Hohenstaufen family, Otto from the Welf family. The Hohenstaufen were also called the Waiblingen, after one of their castles in Swabia. The terms Welf and Waiblingen became Guelf and Ghibelline in Italy. These were the two leading factions in the empire for the next century or so. Pope Innocent III supported Otto of Brunswick after both men had been proclaimed

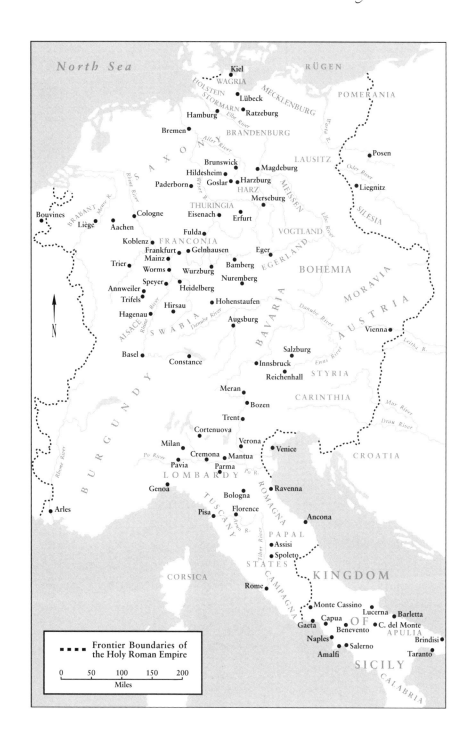

North Sea

RÜGEN

Kiel
WAGRIA
HOLSTEIN
STORMARN
MECKLENBURG
POMERANIA
Lübeck
Hamburg Ratzeburg
Elbe River
Bremen
Aller River
BRANDENBURG

LAUSITZ
Posen
Brunswick Magdeburg
Hildesheim
Oder River
Paderborn Goslar Harzburg Liegnitz
Weser R.
HARZ Merseburg MEISSEN
THURINGIA SILESIA
Bouvines Cologne Eisenach Erfurt
BRABANT Liège Aachen VOGTLAND
Meuse R. Rhine River
Fulda
Koblenz FRANCONIA Eger Elbe River
Frankfurt Gelnhausen
Trier Mainz EGERLAND
Worms Bamberg BOHEMIA
Speyer Wurzburg Nuremberg MORAVIA
Annweiler Heidelberg
Trifels Hirsau Hohenstaufen AUSTRIA
Hagenau Danube River
ALSACE Rhine River SWABIA Augsburg Vienna
BAVARIA Danube River
Basel Salzburg Leitha R.
Constance Innsbruck Enns River
Reichenhall STYRIA
Meran CARINTHIA
Bozen Mur River
Trent Draw River
Cortenuova
Milan Verona Venice
Cremona Mantua CROATIA
Pavia Parma
BURGUNDY Po River Po R.
LOMBARDY
Genoa ROMAGNA Ravenna
Rhone River TUSCANY
Arles Bologna
Pisa Florence Ancona
Arno R.
PAPAL
Tiber River Assisi
Spoleto
STATES KINGDOM
CORSICA CAMPAGNA
Rome
Monte Cassino Lucerna
Capua Barletta
Gaeta C. del Monte
Benevento APULIA
Naples Brindisi
Salerno OF
Amalfi Taranto
SICILY
CALABRIA

**· · · · Frontier Boundaries of
the Holy Roman Empire**

0   50   100   150   200
Miles

German king. This was the beginning of the Guelf party in Italy being associated with the papacy. Ghibellines were considered to be supporters of the empire. This generalization will be useful later in the story, always keeping in mind that local considerations were more important than grand strategic ones.

Philip's support in this dispute came first from the Hohenstaufen lands, in Swabia, in the upper Rhine area of Alsace and Palatine, in the Harz Mountains, and in Switzerland. Otto's main support came from his homeland of Saxony, and the lower Rhine, led by Cologne. Cologne had the strongest links in Germany to England. England, in the person of Richard the Lion-Hearted, had no kind feelings for the Hohenstaufen after his captivity. Otto was also Richard's nephew. Hence, Otto's biggest material support outside Germany came from England, with whom he remained allied until his death.

One of Innocent's goals was to keep the thrones of Sicily and the empire separate. Henry VI combined them in one person, but they were separate thrones. Innocent's ward, Frederick, had the same claim to both thrones. Innocent was willing to allow Frederick to occupy both thrones, but they were to be for separate kingdoms. Innocent was considered one of the founders of the Papal States. The fact that the empire claimed Lombardy and Tuscany in northern Italy, and that the Kingdom of Sicily included most of the southern portions of the peninsula, made any holder of the Papal States nervous when those two areas were ruled by the same person. Land communication between northern and southern Italy had to come through the Papal States, and these areas were always in dispute.

Philip of Swabia also claimed to have rights in the Kingdom of Sicily. Innocent denied those rights, and also denied that Philip had any guardianship interest in Frederick. Philip had continually insisted that he was serving in place of Frederick as emperor. Philip's irritation with Innocent's support of his rival Otto led to an invasion of the Papal States in 1206, led by Liupold, bishop of Worms. Papal forces defeated Liupold's army, and an agreement signed in 1206 by Philip and Innocent confirmed the pope as Frederick's guardian. It also put a stop to Philip's plan to marry Frederick to a daughter of the duke of Brabant as a way to increase Hohenstaufen influence in the Low Countries.

After this settlement with the pope, Philip was in a secure position in the empire. Otto of Brunswick continued to style himself as king as well, and low-level conflict between the two kings continued. However, Philip appeared to be wearing down his opponent slowly. This changed when Otto of Wittelsbach, a discontented suitor for the hand of Philip's daughter, killed Philip in early 1208. Otto of Brunswick was left as the only person who had been elected German king.

Otto, who now styled himself Emperor Otto IV, was in his early thirties. He approved the prosecution of the fugitive Otto of Wittelsbach, who was chased across country and dismembered on the banks of the Danube. With papal approval, Otto IV was betrothed to the eldest daughter of Philip of Swabia, hoping to combine the interests of the Welf and Hohenstaufen into one family. As part of his agreement with Innocent, Otto promised the pope more power in the German church than he had previously exercised. Otto also promised to obey the pope in matters of Italian politics, such as the rule of the Mathildine estates, and rule of several duchies in central Italy.

Otto now appeared to be well set as emperor. It was true that there were some nobles in the empire who continued to wish for a Hohenstaufen to lead them. These nobles were concentrated in what is now southwestern Germany and northern

Switzerland. They lay low for a while, awaiting the result of Otto's trip to Italy to be crowned Holy Roman emperor. Their hope lay with fourteen-year-old Frederick, now trying to navigate the shoals of Sicilian politics and consolidate his status as a king.

THREE

King of Sicily, King of the Romans

F REDERICK TURNED FOURTEEN AT THE END of 1208, and in early 1209, he became king of Sicily in his own right. The resulting first outbreak of disorder started on the island of Sicily. Barons who had obtained parts of the royal lands during Frederick's minority were not happy with his assertion of his rights to that land. Frederick dealt with this by confronting the barons individually, with a squad of troops at his back, and recovering what had been lost. At this point, he did not feel strong enough to reprimand the barons, who under the Norman theory of kingship had committed an act of rebellion, punishable by death. It is not known how he learned the Norman way of kingship, but he showed soon enough that he had.

Frederick also disagreed with the pope about the correct procedure for electing the archbishop of Palermo. Frederick claimed he had the right to confirm the election, under the agreement made between the pope and King Roger I. The pope pointed out that Frederick's mother, Constance, had bargained this authority away during Frederick's minority. The pope also pointed out that the king was getting bad advice. One of his advisers was Walter of Pelear, back in good graces with Frederick.

Innocent negotiated a marriage to Constance of Aragon, recent widow of the king of Hungary. Frederick signed the marriage treaty in Syracuse in early 1209, while on an expedition to pacify that part of Sicily. Constance appeared in August 1209, bringing along the negotiated five hundred knights led by her brother, the count of Provence. Frederick and Constance were married in September 1209, in Palermo. Constance was ten years older than Frederick, and had seen much more of the world than he had. She was also from a leading court in Europe, and her brother was count of an area that was a cultural leader, particularly in poetry, at this time.

Frederick had been described in various letters as a bit of a rough boy before his marriage. He had not spent any time after age four at any royal court. He is described as being very fit, a good horseman, and as ready to exercise with arms as any good knight. However, he did not have good manners. Although his marriage to Constance was a political one, she and her companions did improve Frederick's manners. Later firsthand descriptions of Frederick stress his charm and amiability. Constance fulfilled the first duty of any royal wife in 1210 when she gave birth to a son, named Henry after his Hohenstaufen grandfather. Of all the women in Frederick's life, it appears that he became closest to Constance. She spent more time with him than did his subsequent wives, and when she died he appeared to really mourn, which did not happen at the deaths of his later wives.

Frederick now started the
process of regaining the powers
of a Norman ruler of Sicily. He
had intended to use the five hundred knights brought to his service from Aragon, but most of
them died in an epidemic in
Palermo soon after his wedding.
Frederick then moved to the
mainland and continued asserting
power. He issued an edict com-
manding all landowners to submit their title deeds to the royal
household for examination and
approval. This was greeted with
disdain by barons in Calabria, the
area where Frederick and

Emperor Otto IV meeting Pope
Innocent III. Their relationship
went downhill from here, to
Frederick II's benefit. (*Werkstatt
des Diebold Lauber, Unbekannter
Künstler*)

Constance were residing in 1210. Some of the barons apparently insulted Frederick to his face, and they were imprisoned. This
caused a reaction throughout the domain. Frederick then issued
a circular letter citing the reasons for his action and stressing
that he was well within his legal rights. His subsequent execu-
tion of the barons pushed others into the camp of his new
opponent, Emperor Otto IV.

Otto had come to Italy in 1209 to be crowned Holy Roman
emperor, bringing along an army of German knights. Their
route passed through Lombardy. The Lombard communes
asked Otto to confirm their communal rights as towns. He did
so, and also promised to protect their liberties. He then proceeded into the Mathildine lands and claimed them as part of
the empire. He also issued privileges to towns in the March of

Ancona and Umbria, areas claimed by the pope. Otto met with
Pope Innocent III in Viterbo, just north of Rome, in August
1209. Otto did not concede the lands that the papacy had been
claiming from the empire, but he did concede that the Kingdom
of Sicily was not part of the empire. As a result of this agreement, the pope crowned Otto IV Holy Roman emperor in
Rome on October 4, 1209.

Otto sent some of his army to occupy Tuscany. He had been
in negotiations with the maritime republic of Pisa, which was
urging him to continue south and grant it trading privileges. He
had also been in contact with another of the great survivors of
Italian politics, Dipold of Acerra. Dipold held power in Sicily
before he was ousted by Walter of Pelear. At that time, Dipold
had been captured, but he escaped and fled the kingdom. He
was one of many who persuaded Otto that the Kingdom of
Sicily was part of the empire, an idea that went back at least as
far as Barbarossa. Dipold got his rewards by being made master captain of Apulia and Terra di Lavoro in the Kingdom of
Sicily, and also duke of Spoleto. Spoleto was in the Papal States.
This appointment to offices in the Papal States let the pope
know that Otto was not going to keep his agreements.

Since Barbarossa's time, the papacy feared that
Hohenstaufen rulers would unite the crowns of the empire and
the kingdom, surrounding the Papal States. This had happened
under Henry VI, but he reassured the pope that the crowns
were separate, with them only being held by the same person.
Now the Welfs, in the person of Otto IV, were threatening to
do what the papacy had feared the Hohenstaufen would do.
Otto invaded the mainland portion of the Kingdom of Sicily in
November 1210. Frederick had not yet consolidated his power
in the kingdom, and he retreated to the island of Sicily. Otto
was able to occupy much of southern Italy, and Frederick was

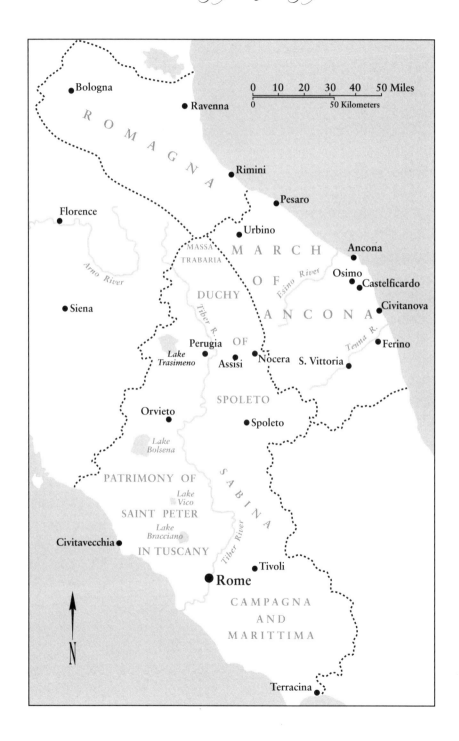

Bologna

Ravenna

R O M A G N A

0   10   20   30   40   50 Miles

0   50 Kilometers

Rimini

Pesaro

Florence

Urbino

MASSA TRABARIA

M A R C H

Ancona

Arno River

O F

Esino River

Osimo

Castelficardo

Siena

DUCHY

A N C O N A

Civitanova

Tiber R.

OF

Tenna R.

Ferino

Perugia

Nocera

S. Vittoria

Lake Trasimeno

Assisi

SPOLETO

Orvieto

Spoleto

Lake Bolsena

S A B I N A

PATRIMONY OF

Lake Vico

SAINT PETER

Lake Bracciano

Civitavecchia

IN TUSCANY

Tiber River

Tivoli

Rome

N

CAMPAGNA

AND

MARITTIMA

Terracina

on the defensive. He had a ship ready to take him to Africa in case Otto was able to make the short jump from the mainland to the island. The Muslims of Sicily had been in contact with Otto, and at this time they opposed Frederick.

Otto appeared to be in a strong position to merge the empire and the kingdom. However, he had serious opponents, both secular and spiritual. Pope Innocent III had been warned by Otto's most formidable opponent, Philip Augustus of France, not to trust Otto. After Otto moved into the Kingdom of Sicily, Innocent excommunicated him in 1211. The pope wrote bishops in Germany that they were released from their oaths of obedience to the emperor. Philip Augustus and Innocent then joined forces by lobbying the German princes to get rid of Otto as emperor. Many of these princes had turned to Otto out of exhaustion after the death of Philip of Swabia, and they were now ready to consider an alternative. Some Lombard towns felt that an emperor present in Italy would suppress their liberties, just after he had confirmed them. Otto was informed of the unrest in Lombardy and Germany, reconsidered his position in southern Italy, and started to withdraw to the north by land starting in November 1211.

Frederick was not in a strong position in November 1211. Otto had conquered, with little trouble or resistance, half of the Sicilian kingdom. The Muslims of the kingdom were united against Frederick, and he had a weak hold on the parts of the island that were not occupied. But Frederick remained calm. He also indulged in a bit of fantasy at this time, adding the symbols of world domination, the sun and moon, to his coat of arms. Considering that his effective rule extended only to parts of the island of Sicily, this seemed a bit optimistic.

At this same time, German princes were meeting in Nuremberg at the urging of Pope Innocent III and Philip

Augustus. They were not happy with Otto, and they voted to depose him. They chose the son of Emperor Henry VI as the new German king. In December 1211, two of their members, Conrad of Ursberg and Anselm of Justingen, were dispatched to inform Frederick of Sicily of his election.

Anselm arrived first in Palermo, in early 1212. He extended the offer, which hopefully meant assuming the imperial crown. Otto, who had withdrawn to northern Italy, would soon hold court at Lodi in Lombardy. He still appeared to have enough of the allegiance of northern Italian towns, and his power base in Germany, to be comfortable in his status as emperor. Otto's minions were putting about the idea that Frederick was merely a tool of the pope, and that the pope had no business interfering with the empire. After his court of Lodi, Otto returned to Germany hoping that all his problems would fade away.

Frederick now faced a difficult, and momentous, decision. He was a new father, Henry being about one year old at this time. He wanted to get Henry crowned king of Sicily, just as Frederick had been crowned while his father was still alive. Frederick's hold on the Kingdom of Sicily was not strong, and many of the mainland barons had already made clear their preference for Otto, particularly if Otto remained far away. Then there was the matter of Frederick's own background. He unquestionably had a German father, but he had never left the territory of the Kingdom of Sicily. What did he know of Germany? The conversations among his advisers can only be imagined. Germans did not have a good reputation in the Kingdom of Sicily. Many people in Sicily wanted to avoid any involvement in German affairs and keep Germans out of Sicilian affairs. As a result, Frederick set out in March 1212 to consult with his old guardian, Pope Innocent III, in Rome.

Innocent still wanted to avoid joining the imperial and Sicilian crowns. However, now he was urging the holder of the Sicilian crown to claim the imperial crown. He asked for assurance that the promises of Frederick's mother, Constance, regarding the relationship of the kingdom and the Holy See would be honored. Innocent also claimed that he had the right to depose emperors, as he had done with Otto, and that he was choosing Frederick to replace him. Innocent recommended Frederick to the Roman people to be acclaimed as emperor, but he did not yet crown him. In exchange for the conditions he had set, Innocent crowned the infant Henry as king of Sicily at the same ceremony that Frederick performed the act of feudal homage to Innocent as his lord for the fief of Sicily. Innocent approved Frederick's decision to leave his wife, Constance, as regent of Sicily, recalled the great survivor Walter of Pelear to court to aid her, and blessed Frederick's trip to claim the crown of the empire. The pope also wrote a message asking any Christian to aid Frederick on his journey to Germany.

Frederick was now ready to set out on the journey to claim the empire. He would take a small entourage with him, but one member of that entourage became very important in Frederick's life. Many historians who commented on Frederick considered him a loner, and not really close to anyone. But one friend who stands out at this time, and who remained close to Frederick until Frederick's death, was a priest, Berard of Castacca. Berard had been a part of the regency council as bishop of Bari during Frederick's minority, and he was now designated papal representative to accompany him. Throughout all the subsequent disputes between Frederick and the papacy, Berard remained loyal to Frederick. Berard eventually became archbishop of Palermo and administered last rites to Frederick on his deathbed.

The next episode of Frederick's life unfolds like a modern adventure movie. Here was a youth of seventeen, with one of the most distinguished bloodlines in Europe, going off with a few companions to claim the crown of the Holy Roman Empire. His assets were few: his name, the backing of the pope, the invitation of some of the princes of the empire, and his own sense of destiny. His goal was to get north of the Alps, where he could try to put these assets to use. He did not have enough money to get there on his own, and many parties in

Pope Innocent III, the pope who raised the medieval papacy to the height of its power. (*Monastero di San Benedetto, Subiaco*)

Italy and the empire wanted to prevent him from ever getting out of Italy. Just leaving Rome and getting to northern Italy presented problems.

Frederick left Rome, traveled about thirty-five miles to Civitavecchia on the west coast of Italy, and sailed for Genoa in a Genoese galley in April 1212. The inveterate rivals of the Genoese, the Pisans, supported Otto, and they had a fleet in the area to try to stop Frederick. This was a continuation of the rivalry of the two cities in Sicily during Frederick's childhood, when the Genoese were able to get Pisans expelled from the kingdom. Despite the Pisan fleet, Frederick landed in Genoa on May 1, 1212. The Genoese welcomed Frederick warmly and commenced to do what they did best: business. Frederick stayed with Niccolo Doria, head of the Ghibelline faction in Genoa, for the next three months. Frederick negotiated a deal with the government of Genoa, borrowing a substantial sum for his expenses to get to Germany. In return, he confirmed the trading rights in Sicily granted to Genoa by Markward, and he promised to pay the Genoese back with 575 pounds of gold. He spent most of his time in Genoa planning his route north.

Northern Italy during the twelfth and thirteenth centuries was a patchwork of communities, some Guelf (supporting first Welfs, then the pope) and some Ghibelline (supporting the Hohenstaufen). Frederick had been invited to some towns, such as Asti, Pavia, and Cremona. Milan had been strongly anti-Hohenstaufen since Barbarossa destroyed it, and continued to be so for all of Frederick's life. Milan detailed some troops to intercept Frederick, aided by a naval contingent from Piacenza that checked barges on the Lombard rivers. Otto had troops stationed at Trent and blocked the normal route north through the Brenner pass. This is what Frederick and his small party faced when they left Genoa in the middle of July 1212.

Frederick was able to make it through Asti to Pavia by July 28. He stayed overnight in Pavia and slipped out of town the next evening after dark. Pavia supplied an armed band of horsemen to escort him to a ford of the Lambro River, where he was to be turned over to an escort from Cremona. Frederick and his party were resting on the bank of the Lambro, waiting for the Cremona troops, when the Milanese discovered them and attacked. Many of the Pavian contingent were killed or captured, but Frederick, who had seen the Cremona troops coming on the other side of the river, grabbed a horse, rode it bareback, and crossed the river to join the Cremona troops. The official historian of Milan stated that "Roger Frederick bathed his bottom in the Lambro."[4] This was true, but Frederick had escaped to the friendly city of Cremona.

4. Van Cleve, *The Emperor Frederick II*, 82.

Northern Italy and Transalpine Europe in the thirteenth century.

From Cremona, Frederick passed through the friendly cities of Mantua and Verona. He had to avoid Bavaria and south Tyrol, whose lords opposed him. Frederick's exact route through the Alps is still unknown, but he was able to get to the Abbey of St. Gall in Switzerland, where he was welcomed by the bishop of Chur. Now Frederick was in Hohenstaufen lands, and the papal message borne by his companion Berard, asking any Christian to aid Frederick on his journey, bore fruit in the raising of some troops supplied by various Swiss abbeys.

Frederick now had three hundred troops available, and he decided to try to beat Otto to the city of Constance in what is now northern Switzerland.

In early August, while Frederick was still riding around in Lombardy, Otto had married Frederick's cousin, Beatrice of Hohenstaufen, with pomp and ceremony. This was his trump card to play against Frederick, combining the two houses. But he did not hold the card long, because Beatrice died under mysterious circumstances before the end of August. Otto set out with his army to intercept Frederick. He was so confident that he sent his cooks into Constance to prepare for his arrival, and these cooks were in the process of preparing an evening meal when something happened to give the meal they were preparing a new owner.

In the various sources I have reviewed, this story is consistent. The one thing missing is the date of the event, but it seems likely that in early September, Frederick heard of Otto's advance to Constance and decided to try to beat him to the punch. Otto was with his army north of Constance in Switzerland, not yet to the bridge he needed to cross, when Frederick showed up with his small force at the southern gate of Constance. The bishop of Constance, the ruler there, was not inclined to let Frederick in. However, an appeal by Berard, stressing that Otto was excommunicate and that Frederick had papal blessing, turned the trick. Although he was unhappy about doing it, the bishop opened the gates and allowed Frederick and his small force into town. The young king showed his leadership skills by summoning the citizens and persuading them to fortify the bridge and deny Otto entry to Constance. He was then able to gain the political allegiance of the town. A French writer of the time, Guillelmus Armoricus, stated that if Frederick had delayed a mere three hours in entering Constance, he would never have won Germany.[5] By evening, however, the town was secure enough that Frederick and his suite were able to enjoy the meal Otto's cooks had prepared in the comfort of Constance.

This whole story borders on the miraculous. Frederick had his great name behind him, but it seems that he felt he was guided by God toward fulfilling his rights and inaugurating a new era in the empire. This may have been the beginning of his conviction that he was the successor to the Roman (not Holy Roman) emperors, and certainly gave him more confidence. The gaining of one city in Germany did not open all the gates to Frederick, but the story spread and led to more support among the German nobles. Frederick was near to the hereditary Hohenstaufen lands of Swabia, where he could count on support. He gained the support of Basel and Strasbourg, and this led him to the upper Rhine, and Swabia. Otto had controlled the upper Rhine in September, and by mid-October he had retreated downriver to his stronghold of Cologne.

Frederick was being acclaimed in southwestern Germany as *puer Sicilia* (boy of Sicily) or *puer Apulia* (boy of Apulia). He was not averse to being characterized as such, to bring out the David and Goliath aspects of his struggle. However, he had to deal with the German princes and the king of France as a presumptive emperor, not a callow child. He met with the son of Philip Augustus of France, soon to be Louis VIII, and made an alliance that stood until Frederick's death. In return for promising not to make peace with the current enemies of France— King John of England and Otto—he received some of the funding he needed to continue to make his progress in Germany.

5. Van Cleve, *The Emperor Frederick II*, 83.

Frederick was now based out of an ancestral castle of the Hohenstaufen at Hagenau in Alsace. This became his favorite residence in the northern portion of his lands, because of the fine hunting in the forests surrounding the castle and because of the library, reputed to be one of the best in Europe.

Many of the lords of the empire had been gathering to greet Frederick, and they held a formal meeting in Frankfurt. On December 5, 1212, Frederick was elected king of the Romans. He was crowned four days later in Mainz, in a ceremony lacking the normal regalia of the emperor, which Otto still possessed.

Frederick had to gather forces to start an active military struggle against Otto. Up to now, the prizes of the empire had fallen in his lap peacefully, with his dramatic appearance from the south. Otto still had a substantial army drawn from his lands in northeastern Germany, and he was allied with his uncle, King John of England (who was also excommunicate at this time); and the duke of Brabant. Frederick's main ally was Philip Augustus of France. Frederick was still gathering his forces when one of the few decisive battles of medieval Europe took place at Bouvines, in what is now Belgium, on July 27, 1214. The forces of Philip Augustus defeated Otto's army, along with a small English force. Otto survived the battle, but his power crumbled, and he had to retreat to his duchy of Brunswick in northeastern Germany.

The diplomacy Frederick had been conducting since late 1212 paid off now. He was able to take an army raised by various princes of the empire from Frankfurt, down the Rhine to the area near the Duchy of Brabant in August 1214. Otto had just married the daughter of the duke of Brabant, and Frederick wanted to make clear that he, Frederick, was the new important power on the scene. Frederick was on the verge of invading the duchy when the duke submitted, gave up his son as a hostage, and acknowledged Frederick as his overlord. Frederick was not able to take either Cologne or Aachen on this trip, but he made it clear that he would return to complete the job the following year.

Frederick returned to Alsace to spend the winter. In the summer of 1215, he set out with his army for Cologne, which fell in June, and for Aachen, which fell in July. Aachen was the ancient seat of Charlemagne and considered the birthplace of the Holy Roman Empire. While his earlier coronation in Mainz as king of the Romans had been legally acceptable, he felt that a coronation in Aachen, at the site of the grave of Charlemagne, using the traditional regalia (which had been recovered from Otto), would demonstrate the reality of his imperial status. Prior to the coronation ceremony, Frederick physically helped to reinter the body of Charlemagne into a great reliquary shrine in the Aachen Cathedral. He then made an announcement after his coronation that greatly affected his life.

Charlemagne was not only considered the father of the Holy Roman Empire, but he was believed to have been an early crusader, the hammer of pagans in eastern Europe and Muslims in Spain. Frederick II's grandfather, Barbarossa, had been on two crusades, dying on the Third Crusade. Frederick's father, Henry VI, was preparing to go on crusade at the time of his death. Frederick had been helped enormously during his struggle to gain the empire by the pope and by church backing in Germany. So after the mass celebrating his coronation was completed, Frederick II took the cross as a crusader. He urged his followers to do so as well, and he never turned his back on this promise. Frederick stated at a later date that this was a chance "to repay God for the many gifts bestowed on us."[6]

6. Van Cleve, *The Emperor Frederick II*, 96.

Frederick did not set off immediately upon taking the cross, as had happened with the People's Crusade of 1096, and the Children's Crusade of 1212, which were somewhat unstructured. He wanted his crusade to be well-organized, and it made more geographical sense to start from Sicily. This started a process of delay that lasted until 1227.

Frederick now had accomplished everything he had set out to do in Germany. He would be the emperor, after a proper coronation in Rome. He had made the Welfs irrelevant, Otto being confined to his duchy of Brunswick, and having no authority outside of it. Frederick now started to act as emperor. He did so in a traditional way. He took no interest in the details of German politics, acting only as an arbiter of disputes between princes of the empire, and providing justice when asked. He confirmed and upheld the rights of the great ecclesiastical and lay princes. Considering his subsequent career as a builder of a strong state and bureaucracy in the Kingdom of Sicily, many German historians have criticized Frederick for missing the chance to turn Germany into a nation-state. This state building was happening at the time in England, France, Spain, and Portugal. Frederick had the ability and will, as he showed in the Kingdom of Sicily.

The main reason Frederick acted this way was that he did not consider himself a German but a Sicilian. He had accepted the idea of the world empire and felt he was the anointed one to bring it into existence. He also felt that the emperor was to be an overlord, not mixed up in the daily business of the people and areas he ruled. Also, he still had good relations with the church, and confirmed ecclesiastical privileges in Germany. He gave concessions to new imperial cities, and let the citizens rule there.

The focus of his activity in Germany was on the empire, not on Germany proper. The empire at this time included what is now Germany; large tracts of what are now Belgium, France, Italy, and Croatia; and the entire lands of what are now Switzerland, Austria, the Netherlands, and the Czech Republic. Frederick delegated power to the rulers already in place and allowed new local institutions to grow up where none existed, such as in areas not yet claimed by any ruler. He wanted to continue the Hohenstaufen line as the emperors, and was trying to get approval of his son, Henry, as his successor. He assured the pope that even though he now wore the crowns of the empire and the Kingdom of Sicily, these realms were combined in crown only.

Frederick's most immediate problem was the continuing existence of Otto as a possible focus of opposition. Frederick continually applied pressure, such as transferring the rule of the province of Schleswig from the duke, a supporter of Otto's, to the Danish king. This restricted Otto still further, as his supporters were now confined to northeast Germany. Otto died in May 1218. He willed to Frederick the main remaining symbol of authority he still had, the crown of Otto the Great, Holy Roman emperor from 962 to 973. Frederick now started the process that would allow him to leave Germany secured and return to the Kingdom of Sicily.

In November 1215, Innocent III reached the zenith of his prestige when he convened the Fourth Lateran Council in Rome, which ratified legislation to centralize the administration of the church in the Roman Curia. Frederick had sent Berard to the council as his representative. Berard did his best to assure the pope and the Curia of Frederick's good intentions.

Frederick's claim to the empire was confirmed by the pope during the meeting of the council. One of the few laymen attending the council was the grand master of the Teutonic Knights, Hermann von Salza. Berard sent a good report about

Hermann to Frederick, who responded by commissioning Hermann to take up the delicate mission of going to see Frederick's wife, Constance, and arranging for her and their son to join Frederick in Germany. This concerned Innocent III, and in a letter dated July 1, 1216, Frederick had to reassure the pope that he did not intend to combine the crowns of the empire and Sicily again. A fortnight later, Innocent III died. Although he and Frederick had disagreed on some things, they had generally had a good relationship. Frederick's relationship with the new pope, Honorius III, would not go as smoothly.

Constance and Henry set out for Germany at about the time Innocent died. They reached Frederick's court later that year, along with Hermann von Salza. Hermann had spent seven years in the crusader states, so he had much to tell Frederick about the politics of where Frederick intended to go on crusade. Hermann so impressed Frederick that he became Frederick's main representative, when needed, to the pope.

Constance briefed Frederick about the situation in the Kingdom of Sicily, which was not good. The mainland barons continued to act as independent lords, and the authority of the king did not extend farther than the island of Sicily. Frederick now concentrated on getting Henry confirmed as his successor for the empire. Henry's name now disappeared from documents in the kingdom, and began showing up in the documents of the empire. Finally, at a meeting of the princes of the empire in Frankfurt in April 1220, Frederick was able to secure Henry's election as German king. In the meantime, he had written Pope Honorius III that he intended to keep the Kingdom of Sicily for himself and rule there. He also said he intended to return to Sicily via Rome, receive the imperial crown from the pope, then set off on crusade.

In order to secure Henry's election, Frederick had had to confirm the rights and privileges of the German princes. This continued the process of fragmenting power in Germany, which was not a major concern of Frederick's. He had now been in the northern part of his empire for eight years, and it was time to return to his home area. He felt he had established his power and consolidated his position as emperor, arranged for the continuing operation of his realm, and assured his succession. This fulfilled his wishes regarding this portion of the empire. Even though he reigned for thirty more years, Frederick returned to Germany only once, for about a year. He spent the rest of his life in Italy and the East, where his true interests lay.

Hermann von Salza, grand master of the Teutonic Knights and diplomat for Frederick II from 1216 until his death in 1239. (*Jan Jerszynski*)

Pope Honorius III, pope from 1216 to 1227. He was the last pope to remain on good terms with Frederick II. (*Basilique Assise, "St. Francis preaching before Honorius III" by Giotto di Bondone*)

FOUR

Crowned as Emperor

IN AUGUST 1220, FREDERICK II gathered his court in Augsburg, the traditional gathering point for any imperial expedition from Germany to Italy. He had been negotiating with Pope Honorius III to be crowned as emperor. Frederick promised that the recent election of his son, Henry, as German king meant the boy was no longer heir to the Kingdom of Sicily, and he vowed to leave Henry in Germany to act as his representative there. Finally, when enough of the continuing disputes between the empire and the anti-imperial communes of northern Italy had been settled, Frederick was able to leave Germany and head south. He left nine-year-old Henry in the care of trusted members of the House of Hohenstaufen, to be raised by others, as Frederick had been. Constance accompanied Frederick, and she never saw her son again.

In early September, Frederick crossed the Alps and entered the plains of Lombardy. The last time he had been in this area he was seventeen and was working (or sneaking) his way north to claim the title of emperor. Now he was returning as one who had been proclaimed emperor five years before and was on his way to the final imperial coronation in Rome. The anti-Hohenstaufen (or Guelf) communes were still suspicious of Frederick, but they had no material grievances at this time. As a result of their opposition during Frederick's trip north, Milan had been under an imperial ban, imposed by Frederick, since 1213. This meant that Milan had no rights to approach the emperor with grievances, and theoretically could not function as a commune. As Frederick's military forces had been in Germany since 1213, no enforcement of the ban was possible. All the communes, including Milan, sent representatives to honor Frederick as he made his way through Lombardy, and he did not attempt to impose his will on the communes. This would have meant imposing local rulers on each individual commune and taking over their collection of tolls and taxes. Frederick may have thought that the Guelf communes were submitting to him, but as we will see, it was really just a cease-fire that lasted until Frederick was safely in southern Italy.

During his journey through Lombardy, Frederick met with emissaries from Venice. They negotiated a commercial agreement between Venice and the empire in return for tribute from Venice. Later, in Bologna, he met with representatives from Genoa, which had aided Frederick on his trip to Germany and had been enjoying trade privileges in all Frederick's lands since then. The Genoese wanted this to continue. Here Frederick showed how he handled matters differently between the empire and the kingdom. He confirmed all Genoese trade privileges in the empire and Lombardy, and allowed them dominion over an increased portion of their adjacent coast. However, he did not confirm their trading rights in the Kingdom of Sicily. He told the Genoese he wished to study the matter after he returned to the kingdom. He also gave the same rights to Genoa's rival, Pisa. Pisa had supported Otto IV and opposed Frederick, but it later changed sides and remained allied to Frederick for the rest of his reign.

Awaiting Frederick in Bologna were papal representatives who raised questions about the separation of the crowns of the empire and the kingdom, and when Frederick was going to go on his crusade. Frederick sent his trusted emissary Hermann von Salza ahead to Rome to negotiate with Pope Honorius III, and continued on his trip south.

Born Cencio Savelli, Honorius III grew up a Roman aristocrat. He became treasurer of the Holy See in 1188, and was made cardinal priest in 1200 by his friend Pope Innocent III. He had been a close associate of Innocent's, and helped develop the policies of crusade and papal overlordship that Innocent propounded. One source states that Frederick had been a pupil of Cencio's in his younger days,[1] but that does not appear in any of the other sources. However, their continuing relationship as pope and emperor-king-crusader shows some of the elements of a teacher and a negligent student. Hermann von Salza's negotiations with the pope were successful, and from his camp outside Rome, Frederick made several promises to reassure the pope. These included a commitment to go on crusade as soon as the affairs of the Kingdom of Sicily were settled, the continued separation of the crowns of the empire and the kingdom, acknowledgement that the kingdom was a fief of the papacy held by Frederick, and a promise that in the kingdom he would use a separate bureaucracy from that of the empire.

1. Masson, *Frederick II of Hohenstaufen*, 60–61.

The imperial coronation took place November 22, 1220, in St. Peter's Church. Several previous coronations had been accompanied by riots in Rome, but not this one. The ceremony went well, and the new emperor was displayed before the Roman people, mitered, and crowned, carrying all the symbols of his right to rule, showing his universal authority. He then held the stirrup of the pope's horse for the pope to mount, and led the mounted horse for a few steps. Barbarossa thought this ritual was demeaning and had to be talked into performing it, but Frederick II took it in stride.

Frederick had reaffirmed his crusading vow. As a result of Pope Innocent's earlier call to crusade, an expedition was in Damietta in Egypt at this time. Honorius III wanted Frederick to aid this effort. They agreed that Frederick would leave in August 1221, and also send immediate financial and military help to Damietta. Frederick also confirmed the liberties of the church he had guaranteed in the empire. This was contained in an imperial decree, *Constitutio in Basilica Beati Petri*, issued in celebration of his coronation. The decree condemned heretics and confirmed the emperor's ties to the church. The secular dimension of the decree was meant to state the emperor's intention to offer peace and security to all his subjects. This decree summarized his imperial policy, spiritual and secular. Frederick wanted to protect his subjects and their rights, and honor the church.

ORGANIZING THE KINGDOM OF SICILY

Frederick now returned to the Kingdom of Sicily, a short trip south from Rome. During his absence, Constance and then the regency council she had left behind had done the best they could to keep order in the kingdom. However, the barons had done their best to reassert the rights they had exercised since the death of Henry VI. They seized royal lands, and royal authority had diminished, particularly in the southern mainland. Frederick may have been thinking hard about this state of affairs on his trip south, because on reaching the first major town in the kingdom, Capua, he acted to correct matters.

In December 1220, Frederick issued a series of decrees that have come to be known as the Assizes of Capua. These decrees applied only to the kingdom and were an attempt to turn the clock back to the time of Frederick's cousin William II. Frederick insisted that any privileges issued since 1189 be turned in to the crown for scrutiny. Several other Western rulers had taken such action since the beginning of the twelfth century, such as Henry II and Richard I of England, and Roger II of Sicily. This move gave the king a double opportunity. On one hand, he could regain lands, enhancing the crown's fiscal and military position, and also award some land back to supporters. On the other hand, if he did confirm the rights and privileges as they existed, a substantial fee was charged, profiting the crown. No military struggles resulted from these decrees.

The decrees were also meant to reinstate the Norman system of justice as it had been conducted under Frederick's forebears Roger II, William I, and William II. Some of the Campanian and Apulian towns had since been granted generous privileges by Markward or Tancred, which they were still exercising. Frederick announced that these towns were now to be reintegrated into the kingdom's system of justice and finance. He brought the customs system under royal control, as it had slipped away during his minority and absence. All roads and ports were to be under royal protection and sanction. There was a clear financial motive in all these rulings. Frederick had been able to get along in the empire with contributions and fees collected from the leading princes and from privileges granted to smaller principalities and cities. However, in the kingdom, financial responsibility was centralized in the monarchy, not dispersed to the nobility, and Frederick intended that Sicily would retake her place as one of the most prosperous states in Europe.

The international effect of the Capua assizes became clear in Frederick's dealings with Genoa. The decrees left no place for the Genoese claims to special status. Genoa had treated the town of Syracuse on the island of Sicily as a colony, imposing its own tax system and using it as a base to conquer Crete. In the next two years, Frederick proceeded to rid the kingdom of Genoese influence and presence. The leaders of Syracuse and surrounding areas were kicked out, their property was expropriated, the warehouses seized and sold off. Frederick knew that the way to deal with Genoa's anger was to become friendly with its rivals, Pisa and Venice. He did not give Genoa's old privileges to Pisa and Venice, but made them all equal in the eyes of the kingdom and the empire. Genoa moved into the Guelf camp in northern Italy, but Frederick felt that the financial gains in the kingdom made this worthwhile.

After his stop in Capua, Frederick continued a zigzag course throughout his south Italian domains. It appears this is when he spent his first substantial amount of time in Apulia, which became his favorite part of the kingdom. Legend has it that during this visit to Apulia, Frederick had a personal meeting in Bari with the leading ascetic of the day, Francis of Assisi. This is possible, because Francis was returning from crusade in Egypt at this time. Supposedly, the skeptical emperor tried to tempt Francis by introducing a beautiful woman into his bedroom, and watched the proceedings through a keyhole. One version of the story says that Francis called down from heaven a fiery shield to drive off the woman. Another says Francis put the coals from the brazier on the floor, lay on the coals, and asked the woman to join him. In both stories, the woman flees. Regardless of the truth of the legend, both Frederick and Francis, for very different reasons, spent much of their lives fighting the riches and corruption of the church.

Frederick's final destination was the island of Sicily. He reached Messina in spring 1221. New decrees were issued there, based on Norman, Roman, and canon law. Some of the decrees were minor, such as laws against gambling and employment of jesters at noble courts. Some decrees dealt with Jews. In the empire, Frederick had declared Jews as "serfs of the royal chamber," meaning they were under his protection. In the kingdom, Jews were to wear distinctive clothes, and males were to grow their beards. In 1231, legislation was issued to protect money-lending by Jews. Prostitutes were also regulated in 1221. Frederick apparently felt that prostitutes, like Jews, were non-Christian and needed to be regulated in a Christian state. These decrees did not deal with the largest non-Christian group in the kingdom, the Muslims. As we will see, Frederick had different plans for them.

Later that year, on June 23, Empress Constance died in Catania. She was buried in Palermo, and Frederick showed real grief at her death, supposedly placing his own crown on her head prior to burial. They had been married since 1209, and it appears that Constance was the only woman Frederick treated with real respect in his adult life. He had left her as regent in the kingdom when he went north, and he eventually called for her to join him in 1216. Since then, they had been living together as husband and wife. This did not result in any more children from Constance, but it did appear to tighten their bonds of affection. She was the only one of Frederick's wives crowned empress. Like most other rulers in the thirteenth century,

Frederick took lovers and had several illegitimate children. He acknowledged and raised these children, and some of them played important parts in the rest of his story.

The island of Sicily had a large Muslim population, which had been essentially autonomous in western Sicily until William II gave their land to the abbey of Monreale. William also increased the pressure on Muslims to convert, which led to an increased number of converts (though mostly to Greek Orthodoxy rather than Roman Catholicism) and a revolt of the remaining Muslims. So a guerrilla war had been going on since about the time of Frederick's birth against the ecclesiastical authorities of Monreale and the central administration of the kingdom. The Muslims had shown themselves to be powerful in western Sicily, near their main area of Girgenti and the surrounding mountains. They were also in contact with North African Arabic rulers, who supplied arms, funds, and men.

Frederick was thought to be more sympathetic to Muslims than most other Christian leaders of the time. However, the challenge to his rule was too much, so he moved against the Muslims by attacking their strongholds. One of their leaders, ibn Abbad, was seized and brought before Frederick, whereupon he fell on his face and begged his pardon. Frederick dug his spur into the side of the rebel and tore his body open. Ibn Abbad survived, only to be hanged a week later in Palermo along with two merchants of Marseilles who had been caught aiding the Muslims. This broke the organized revolt in Sicily. Frederick seized Jerba, an island off the coast of Tunisia that had been supplying the rebels and was also a nest of pirates. He expelled Muslims from the island, leaving the large Jewish community there as the main residents. He urged other Jews to migrate there and aided them. This was the extent of Frederick's actions in North Africa at the time.

The fortress of Lucera, the Muslim enclave on the mainland of Italy, established by Frederick II, in 1225, which remained Muslim until 1300. (*Art of Falconry [1943]*)

The rebellion of the Muslims in southwestern Sicily continued at a low, guerrilla level. The Muslims were spread out over a large area and were difficult to control. Frederick wanted to move on with his administration of the rest of the kingdom and with his promised crusade. He came up with a new solution for his time: gathering all the Muslims together and relocating them to one spot. He selected the town of Lucera, an old Byzantine settlement in the mainland province of Apulia. Lucera was to be a special Muslim enclave. As many Muslims as could be captured were deported there during the rest of the 1220s, eventually leading to a town of about fifteen thousand, a sizable community by thirteenth-century standards.

Frederick allowed and encouraged the practice of Islam at Lucera, while demanding the payment of a poll tax, which had been initiated by Muslim rulers and levied on Christians and Jews. Frederick used it in the Norman manner, levying it on Muslims and Jews, while not interfering in their religious practices. Muslim law was allowed in Lucera, again in the prior Norman tradition. Frederick came to like Lucera quite a lot, building a palace there in the 1230s in a recognizably Oriental style. Many of Frederick's practices and policies contradicted those of William II, who discontinued the reception of Muslims at court and originated the policy of conversion. Frederick was aware of the religious devotion of the Muslims in the kingdom, as they had fought for over 150 years to retain their faith. He made Muslims "serfs of the chamber" in order to take advantage of their abilities, as he had done with the Jews.

In the case of the Muslims, the skills Frederick was interested in were military. A Muslim bodyguard was formed that traveled with Frederick to the Holy Land. Other units were formed to serve as light cavalry and archers in his army. Whether this policy was an example of "rare enlightenment"[2] or "using them for practical purposes,"[3] the problem of Muslims as an autonomous political body in the kingdom had been solved, and there was no separate history of Islam in Sicily after the relocation to Lucera.

Frederick wanted to get the system of justice in the kingdom under his control. This involved appointing justiciars, who were empowered to travel a circuit in the kingdom. On this circuit they heard disputes and made decisions that were binding on the parties. Justiciars had a history in the kingdom since the time of Count Roger I in the early twelfth century. Then, justiciars had mostly been resident nobles who handled justice in their own lands. But there had been a gradual shift to more professional, nonresident justiciars. One of Frederick's decrees even made it illegal for a justiciar to own land in the area of his

2. Van Cleve, *The Emperor Frederick II*, 153.
3. David Abulafia. *Frederick II: A Medieval Emperor* (London, 1988), 148.

administration. Still, there was a shortage of able, nonnoble personnel to fulfill these functions. Frederick took steps to remedy the situation for the long term by founding the University of Naples in 1224. The university was to emphasize legal studies, and students from the kingdom were prohibited from going to Bologna (the existing center for legal studies in Italy) and required to go to Naples. Frederick appointed as many qualified nonnobles as he could. The remaining posts were filled by nobles, who had to obey the nonresident law. (The University of Naples has operated since 1224, continuing its emphasis on legal studies. It and a preexisting school in Salerno that was known for medical studies were useful in supplying qualified professionals to the kingdom.)

Frederick still had not honored his promise to lead the next crusade. He was continually reminded of it by Pope Honorius III, who had already suffered through the failure of the Damietta expedition in 1221. Frederick and the pope discussed the launching of Frederick's promised crusade at a meeting at Ferentino in March 1223. Many other interested parties were there, including the titular king of Jerusalem, John of Brienne; the Latin patriarch of Jerusalem; and the leaders of the three military orders: the Knights Templar, the Knights Hospitaller, and the Teutonic Knights. Hermann von Salza, Frederick's trusted associate, had been promoting the idea of Frederick marrying the daughter of John of Brienne, Isabella. John claimed to be king of Jerusalem, but this was only based on the fact that he was married to the queen, Mary of Jerusalem, who had inherited the title from her father. The legitimate title had passed to her daughter, Isabella. The marriage was finally agreed to at Ferentino, along with a definite date of departure for Palestine of 1225. Frederick had been building the ships necessary for awhile and hoped to have them all ready by then.

Frederick committed himself to fund all the personnel who became part of his crusade, avoiding the financial problems that had plagued the Damietta crusade. The pope agreed to Frederick's funding the crusade and sent John of Brienne to northern Europe to gather participants, along with preachers to aid John in his recruiting.

The response to the appeal to crusade was not good. Some knights committed themselves, but they would not be coming south for awhile. After the pope reviewed the progress made by the preachers in the north, and the emperor reviewed his gathering of money and ships, another meeting was held between representatives of the emperor and the pope at San Germano in early 1225. Pope Honorius realized that the crusade would not be ready by 1225, and he wanted to ensure its success. So an agreement was reached to delay the departure to 1227. The size of the force (two thousand cavalry) and the funds (625 pounds of gold) to be supplied by the kingdom were set as well. Honorius promised to excommunicate Frederick if this deadline was not met, and he continued to urge him to hurry. Many in the Curia thought Honorius was not being firm enough with Frederick, and a propaganda campaign was started against the emperor. This campaign was led by a long-time enemy of Frederick's, Ugo, the cardinal bishop of Ostia.

Isabella of Jerusalem was married to Frederick in a proxy ceremony in Acre in Palestine, with the archbishop of Capua as Frederick's representative. Isabella was then crowned queen of Jerusalem at a ceremony in Tyre. Frederick's fleet then carried her back to the kingdom for the official marriage. The ceremony took place in Brindisi on November 9, 1225. Isabella had been reluctant to leave her homeland, but she obeyed her father's wishes. She was accompanied by a large suite, including a train of ladies. Several sources indicate that Frederick was not pleased to be married to a girl of fifteen. He became enamored of a member of Isabella's suite who was thought to be a cousin of Isabella's and a distant cousin of Frederick's. Whether this is true or not, it is clear that Frederick left Isabella immediately after the ceremony and did not live with her as husband and wife much throughout their marriage. Frederick started to style himself as king of Jerusalem after the wedding, to the fury of John of Brienne, now his father-in-law. John became a consistent foe of Frederick's and went to the papal court to spread this opposition.

The marriage of Frederick II and Isabel of Jerusalem. Isabel was the legitimate queen of the Kingdom of Jerusalem. This marriage allowed Frederick II to style himself king of Jerusalem. (*British Library*)

Frederick was still serious about going on crusade, although he had matured greatly from the twenty-year-old who took crusading vows in 1215. He intended to gather more support for the crusade from the empire, so he called an imperial diet to meet in the strongly Ghibelline town of Cremona at Easter 1226. His purpose was to gather the great lords of the northern empire and the communes from Lombardy and discuss the expedition to the East. Many of the lords of the northern empire, including his son, Henry, set off to attend the meeting. Even though it had been made clear that the meeting had nothing to do with the state of affairs in northern Italy, many of the Guelf towns did not believe this. Led by Milan, some of these communes decided at a meeting in Mantua to refound the Lombard League, which had been dissolved at the end of hostilities with Barbarossa in 1183. The communes promised to hold together for twenty-five years in resistance to any reduction in their rights by the emperor. They also sent troops to the mountain passes and prevented many German princes, including Henry, from getting through the Alps to attend the meeting.

The meeting went forward anyway. Frederick kept himself to requests that were legitimate under the Treaty of Constance from 1183. He wanted to appeal for help on the crusade. However, now that organized opposition had shown itself, he felt he needed to assert authority over the communes in the Lombard League. Most had attended the diet, but Milan did not send a delegation. Before taking any military action against the members of the league, Frederick discussed the situation with the cardinal of Porto, the papal representative at the diet. The cardinal, who wanted to get the crusade going, decided to mediate the dispute. An agreement was reached in August that required the Lombard League, which was allowed to remain in existence, to supply four hundred cavalry and to prosecute religious heretics. The emperor took no remedial action against his rebellious subjects. Still the league delayed complying with the agreement, and Honorius was forced to threaten to use the interdict—the exclusion of an entire geographical area from Christian sacraments and burial—and excommunication against its leaders. The agreement was finally signed in March 1227.

The agreement was sent back to Rome for approval, which came from a new pope. Honorius III had died in mid-March 1227. He had tried to keep the peace in Europe by conciliating and cooperating with the emperor. Honorius had approved the foundation of the Dominican and Franciscan orders during his reign and did not impose his will on the emperor. He was very interested in the crusade and had made clear that he expected

Frederick to honor his vows regarding it. Even though the new pope approved the agreement between Frederick and the Lombard communes, the election of Ugo of Ostia, who took the name Gregory IX, would mean a great change in papal-imperial relations.

Pope Gregory IX was the first papal opponent of Frederick.
(*Syracuse University Library*)

FIVE

Crusader

Pope Gregory IX was born sometime before 1171 to the family of the count of Segni, and he was baptized Ugo. After studying at the University of Paris, he was tapped by his uncle, Pope Innocent III, to work as a diplomat representing Innocent. Ugo was involved in negotiations with Markward of Anweiler as far back as 1198, and had also been appointed papal representative in Germany. Hence, Ugo was familiar with both realms held by Frederick II. Ugo was named cardinal bishop of Ostia in 1206, which made him a powerful member of the Vatican Curia. He was an enthusiastic supporter of Pope Innocent III's assertion of papal power and influence. He was also a truly religious man, a friend of both Francis of Assisi and Dominic, and he assisted both of them in getting the mendicant orders of Franciscans and Dominicans recognized by Pope Honorius III.

Ugo started out as a supporter of Frederick. He was present when Frederick reaffirmed his crusader vows in Rome at his coronation. But Ugo lost patience with the various delays, and, as a close adviser to Honorius, he counseled Honorius to take firmer action against Frederick. By the time of Honorius's death, Ugo was the leader of the anti-Frederick faction in the Curia. After his election as Gregory IX, he approved the agreement between Frederick and the Lombard League. Gregory set a deadline for Frederick to leave on the crusade by September 1227, renewing Honorius's threat of excommunication if this deadline was not met.

MAKING PREPARATIONS

Frederick was proceeding with his preparations to leave for the East. The preparations were twofold: gathering men and ships in the kingdom, and negotiating with the Egyptian leader al-Kamil. In the history of the Crusades, there were two types of expeditions to the East—the popular, enthusiastic crusades, and the aristocratic, professional crusades. Frederick wanted his expedition to be one of the latter. His gathering of forces was intended to secure knights with their required support personnel, not the sizable crowds that had marked the popular Crusades. Frederick's method of encouraging aristocratic participation was to help the knights economically. Frederick had spread the word for the last couple of years that he would pay for the transport to the Holy land, which had always been the largest expense for any knight. This crusade had been discussed for several years, and the deadline of 1227 was known. Hence, Frederick had gathered a good-sized group of knights and retainers in Apulia in late summer 1227 who were prepared to leave soon for the East. One large group of German knights was led by the landgrave of Thuringia, an old supporter of Frederick from his time in Germany.

Frederick had been exploring the situation and personalities of the Holy Land for quite some time. He did not intend to show up with his army and bludgeon his way to retaking Jerusalem. The Kingdom of Jerusalem claimed by Frederick consisted of the coast of Palestine from just north of Beirut to just south of Jaffa. Jerusalem had been part of this kingdom but had been lost in 1187. Frederick had shown more of an ability to achieve goals by diplomacy and persuasion rather than by brute force. His takeover of the Holy Roman Empire was accomplished that way. His imposition of rule in the Kingdom of Sicily did involve some use of force, but it was mostly accomplished by his presence and use of personal power. He knew that to do this in the Holy Land, he had to be informed as to the political and military situation on the ground. His two main sources were John of Brienne, who was now an opponent, and his loyal supporter Hermann of Salza. Hermann had returned to Germany and gathered a force of knights from the Teutonic Order, and he intended to accompany Frederick on his trip to the Holy Land.

Unlike prior crusaders, Frederick had established diplomatic ties with a leader in the Muslim world of the Near East before setting off. At this time, the Muslim-held lands between Syria and Egypt were divided between the successors to the great leader Saladin. Al-Kamil held Egypt and part of Palestine, and his brother and enemy, al-Malik, held Syria and other parts of Palestine. Al-Kamil initiated contact with Frederick, as explained by Muslim historian ibn Wasil: "The idea of the approaches made to the emperor, the king of the Franks, and of his invitation, was to create difficulties for al-Malik al-Mu'azzam [of Damascus] and to prevent his availing himself of the help offered to him by the sultan Jalal ad-Din ibn 'Ala ad-Din Khwarizmshah and Muzaffar ad-Din of Arbela, in his quarrel with al-Kamil."[1]

Frederick then contacted al-Malik and asked what he would offer Frederick to prevent him from marching on Jerusalem. Al-Malik's reply was one word: war. So Frederick proceeded with his contacts with al-Kamil. The Egyptian leader sent an emissary to Frederick's court in 1226. The court in Cairo must have had some knowledge of Frederick, because the emissary sent, Emir Fakhr ad-Din, was a man after Frederick's own heart: he was intellectually curious about the mysteries of the universe, and was a fine horseman and expert falconer. Their negotiations led Frederick to send an embassy to Cairo, led by Archbishop Berard of Palermo and Frederick's current representative in the Holy Land, Count Thomas of Acerra. Frederick asked for custody of Jerusalem, and al-Kamil said he would support Frederick in that matter but that al-Malik now held it. They agreed that Frederick would attack al-Malik and eventually be rewarded with a reconstituted Kingdom of Jerusalem.

This is where things stood in late summer of 1227. The crusaders were gathered in Apulia for their departure, which was to be from the port of Brindisi in September. However, the crowded camps in summertime southern Italy bred disease, and a virulent infection, probably typhoid or cholera, spread among the crusaders. Frederick knew that this was a major complication, but he still felt he had to proceed. The fleet sailed by the end of September. Soon afterward, the disease struck on Frederick's ship. He and the landgrave of Thuringia were both afflicted. The landgrave died, and Frederick became seriously

1. David Abulafia. *Frederick II: A Medieval Emperor* (London, 1988), 171.

ill. Since he could not supply the leadership necessary in his state, he sent some ships ahead under the duke of Limburg and Hermann von Salza. The troops were to go to Cyprus, and then on to the coastal area of the Kingdom of Jerusalem to await the emperor's arrival, hopefully the following year. Frederick and the rest of the fleet returned to Otranto, in the kingdom.

On his return, Frederick went to rest and seek a cure at the baths of Pozzuoli, and he sent ambassadors to Pope Gregory with his explanation. Gregory had been waiting for such an opportunity. In October, after being notified of what had happened, he issued an encyclical letter with many grievances against Frederick. The letter did not just state that Frederick broke his crusading promise but also listed

This drawing of Frederick and al-Kamil (right) is imagined as they never met. (*Cronaca del Villani; detail*)

such complaints as his treatment of the church in the kingdom, Frederick's holding the crowns of the kingdom and the empire, and other grievances. A subsequent letter detailed more charges and publicized Frederick's excommunication, which one historian has called "an occupational hazard of medieval emperors."[2] I would change that to medieval rulers. Examples of rulers who were excommunicated around this time include Barbarossa, Otto IV, and King John of England. Many other rulers were excommunicated during and after Frederick's lifetime.

2. David Abulafia. *Frederick II: A Medieval Emperor* (London, 1988), 167.

Frederick responded to the excommunication by issuing a letter addressed to all who had taken the cross with him. He explained what he had done for the current expedition, promising to lead it again the following year. He issued a letter to fellow rulers, denying papal claims of overlordship and criticizing the popes as money-grubbers. He also accused the church of abandoning its own ideals.

The two competing views of the pope and the emperor were now on public display for the literate of the day. At Easter 1228, the populace of Rome showed whose side it was on. Pope Gregory preached a sermon against Frederick at St. Peter's, and the congregation rewarded him with a riot. Gregory had to flee fifteen miles to Viterbo. By this time it was clear that Frederick intended to proceed with the crusade without papal blessing. The pope's disapproval had not hindered his ability to gather money or forces.

Before Frederick could leave for the East, two major events affected what he wanted to do there. First, the cause of al-Kamil's invitation to Frederick to come East, his dispute with his brother al-Malik, was removed when al-Malik died in early 1228. Frederick was informed of this before leaving but decided to continue with his expedition. Al-Kamil now had no reason to give up Jerusalem without a fight.

The second major event, which was positive for Frederick's claim to the Kingdom of Jerusalem, came in April 1228, when Isabella gave birth to a son, Conrad. She died soon afterward, and Frederick showed no signs of sorrow at her death. Isabella had been the legitimate queen of Jerusalem, and Frederick was her consort. The title of king or queen of Jerusalem could pass through the female line. Now Frederick was the father of the legitimate king of Jerusalem, a title Conrad inherited on Isabella's death. Conrad would be in no position for at least fifteen years to influence any actions Frederick took in his place. Conrad's birth also weakened the position of John of Brienne, as Conrad's claim to the crown was superior to John's. Frederick continued to call himself king of Jerusalem, even though he agreed it was Conrad who held the legitimate claim.

It was becoming clear that Pope Gregory was preparing to launch a war against the kingdom on Frederick's departure. Still, Frederick continued preparations to leave for the East. Gregory sent a papal representative to Germany to see if there was any organized opposition to Frederick there, but he found none.

On his departure in May 1228, Frederick sent a mission to the pope, stating that he had now fulfilled his vow. Gregory rejected this and responded by saying Frederick's disgrace was now compounded. He was an impenitent, excommunicated crusader, a contradiction in terms. The ground was now set for an attack by a pope on the domain of a king who was away on crusade.

EXPEDITION TO THE HOLY LAND

Frederick's fleet left Brindisi on June 28, 1228. His force consisted of about one thousand five hundred knights supported by about ten thousand infantry. Included in the infantry were some Muslim units Frederick had formed after the establishment of Lucera. Frederick allowed these Muslims the open practice of their religion, which did not please the reverend archbishops who accompanied the crusade.

Frederick knew that even with the support he would gain from the crusader orders in the Holy Land, his force would not be large enough to accomplish its goals solely by military means. He continued to negotiate with al-Kamil, and he placed more faith in diplomacy than in force.

The first stop for the fleet was Cyprus, which it reached on July 21, 1228. Cyprus had been an imperial fief since the days of Frederick's father. The current king, Henry Lusignan, was a child. The real ruler of the island was John of Ibelin, lord of Beirut, the richest noble in the Kingdom of Jerusalem. Frederick called for Henry, John, and the other nobles resident in Cyprus to meet him in Limassol for a great banquet in preparation for the departure to the Holy Land. During the banquet, Frederick had armed soldiers come in and stand behind each of the nobles. He asked for John to hand over Beirut, and to hand over the income of Cyprus for the past ten years. John resisted.

After some bluster, Frederick and John turned to the issue at hand: the conquest of the Holy Land. Frederick backed off his demands for money at this point, but he took hostages from the Ibelin party into his service for the duration of the crusade. Although Frederick had shown he was an opponent of John's, John behaved correctly as a subject of the emperor's, discouraging some knights who asked for his help in a plot to assassinate Frederick. He accompanied Frederick on the expedition to the Holy Land and rendered good service.

Frederick was not clear in his own mind about the situation that had developed in the Christian East. Due to early deaths of its rulers, there had been a series of royal minorities in the Kingdom of Jerusalem, like the one in place now for Conrad. This weakened the authority of that crown enormously, to the benefit of the local barons. Frederick sent letters to the princes of the neighboring crusader states of Antioch and Tripoli, asking them to submit to his rule. They refused.

Frederick was trying to impose his imperial will more directly than he had done in Germany, and he was being thwarted. He had some supporters among nobles in Cyprus, who accompanied him to the mainland. His enemies decided to lay low at this point and wait for him to complete his mission and return to the Kingdom of Sicily.

This return was also on Frederick's mind. Pope Gregory had started his campaign against the Kingdom of Sicily soon after Frederick left for the crusader states. But Frederick felt that he needed to prove to the pope and his companions on crusade that he had fulfilled his crusader vows before he returned.

On September 7, 1228, Frederick arrived in Acre in the Kingdom of Jerusalem. He was greeted with acclamation by the populace and, more importantly, by the Templars and Hospitallers. Even the patriarch of Jerusalem consulted with Frederick, while banning him from religious services as an excommunicate. This force in Palestine was meant to impress al-Kamil, but not to bring him to battle. After landing in Acre, Frederick sent an embassy to al-Kamil, headed by Thomas of Acerra and a Syrian baron, Bailan of Sidon, bearing lavish gifts and Frederick's proposals. They reached al-Kamil while he was in Nablus, conducting a campaign against Damascus. Al-Kamil had deposed the young son of his brother and was trying to establish control in the territories al-Malik had held. Al-Kamil did not want Frederick in the Holy Land, but he was there, with an army, and had to be dealt with.

While Frederick paraded his army down the coast from Acre to Jaffa, the negotiations continued. Neither sovereign wanted to fight, and Frederick made the case that Jerusalem was less important to al-Kamil than was Damascus. Frederick stressed that Jerusalem was a worn-out city that was more important to Christianity than to Islam, and he proposed to tear down its walls and make it an open city. Frederick was in a great hurry to finish an agreement, and the final treaty was transmitted from al-Kamil to Frederick on February 11, 1229. Fakhr ad-Din, who had come to know Frederick on his embassy to Sicily, played a role in convincing al-Kamil of the benefits of the agreement. The final treaty was accompanied by many gifts for the emperor, such as jewels, camels, Arabian mares, and an elephant.

The final agreement was a ten-year truce. Jerusalem was to be turned over to the Kingdom of Jerusalem but to remain unfortified. The Temple Mount was to be excluded from Christian control, as it was home to two of the holiest places in Islam, the al-Aqsa mosque and the Dome of the Rock. Hebron and other areas in the vicinity of Jerusalem were to remain in Muslim hands. There would be a narrow corridor between Jerusalem and the sea that would be in Christian control. Bethlehem and Nazareth were handed over to the Kingdom of Jerusalem, with appropriate corridors to connect them with the rest of the kingdom. The most important shrines of Christianity, the places of Annunciation, Nativity, and Crucifixion, were placed in Christian hands, along with the Church of the Holy Sepulchre. The resulting map was filled with enclaves and corridors that might remind readers in the early twenty-first century of the current situation and proposed solutions in Palestine.

As often seems to be the case throughout history, this treaty avoiding military conflict was seen on both sides as a betrayal.

On the Christian side, all prior crusades, even though they included some diplomacy, had been military expeditions. All had resulted in some fighting, and in some atrocities committed by both sides. When the First Crusade had conquered Jerusalem, the result for the residents was a bloodbath. The current result was more to Frederick's taste. This expedition had been carried out in an organized, rather than an emotional way. He did not feel that battles in the hinterlands of Syria, which was where al-Kamil's army was, would serve the purpose of gaining

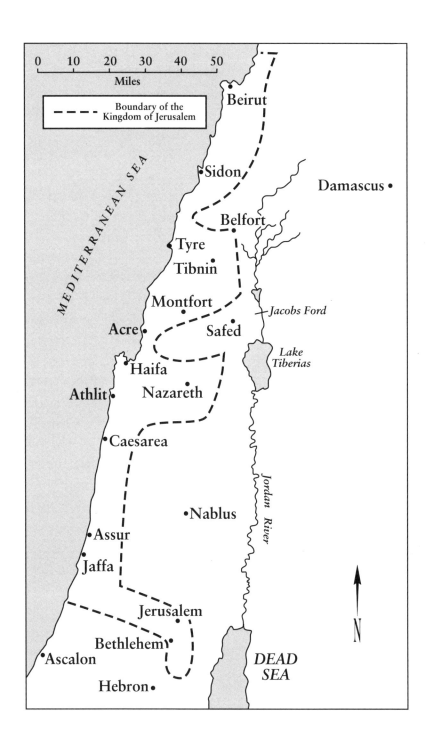

0 10 20 30 40 50
Miles

– – – Boundary of the
Kingdom of Jerusalem

MEDITERRANEAN SEA

•Beirut

•Sidon

Damascus •

•Belfort

•Tyre

Tibnin

Montfort

— *Jacobs Ford*

Acre•

Safed•

*Lake
Tiberias*

•Haifa

Athlit•

Nazareth•

•Caesarea

•Nablus

Jordan River

•Assur

Jaffa•

Jerusalem•

Bethlehem•

•Ascalon

Hebron•

*DEAD
SEA*

N

Jerusalem, the object of the crusade. But the barons of the crusader states were furious that they had been left out of the negotiating process. And the patriarch of Jerusalem condemned the treaty as having no value, especially noting the condition that the holy places of Islam remained in Muslim control.

The Muslim opponents of the treaty were also vocal. Al-Kamil pointed out to them that Islamic law provided for a maximum truce with infidels of ten years, ten months, ten weeks, and ten days. He intended to consolidate his power by then and recover the unfortified Jerusalem, which he said would be an easy fruit to pluck at the end of the truce. Al-Kamil's opponents said that he had given up, and that the treaty prohibited Muslim pilgrims from visiting Jerusalem. This belief, while not true, stiffened the determination of the besieged occupants of Damascus for the short term.

On March 17, 1229, Frederick reached Jerusalem. The pilgrims who had accompanied the crusade followed him to the city, but many of the religious leaders did not, to avoid dealing with an excommunicate. The main focus of all the Christians was the Church of the Holy Sepulchre, which had not been harmed during the Muslim occupation. Frederick was greeted by the *qadi*, or religious judge, of Nablus, appointed by al-Kamil to be Frederick's host. The *qadi*, out of respect for the change of power in Jerusalem, had instructed the muezzins not to give their normal call to prayer in the evening. The next day, Frederick is reported to have inquired why the call had not been given. The *qadi* said he had prevented it, out of respect for Frederick. Frederick replied, "My chief aim in passing the night in Jerusalem was to hear the call to prayer given by the muezzins, and their cries of praise to God during the night."[3]

3. David Abulafia. *Frederick II: A Medieval Emperor* (London, 1988), 185.

This story may be apocryphal. It was reported in Muslim sources, who did not understand Frederick's interest in their religion and seeming lack of interest in his own.

On his second day in Jerusalem, Frederick attended mass in the Church of the Holy Sepulchre. During the mass, he wore the crown as king of Jerusalem. After the service, a speech was delivered on his behalf, in German, to the congregation, which consisted mostly of Teutonic knights. Frederick reviewed his actions since taking the cross in Aachen in 1215, to the successful conclusion the previous day. He was aware of the opposition of the pope and church authorities. He pleaded for reconciliation, claiming he was subordinate to God and wished to deal with Gregory IX on that basis. He did not address the now-restored Kingdom of Jerusalem but dealt with larger issues.

Frederick was different from the prior crusaders the Muslims had dealt with. He was genuinely interested in Muslim architecture, philosophy, science, and belief. According to one story, while visiting the Temple Mount, Frederick spotted a priest going into the al-Aqsa mosque with a Bible. Frederick forbade his entry, out of respect for the devotions of the Muslims.[4]

Frederick had discussions with Islamic leaders, who recorded their impressions of him. They were unimpressed with him physically, saying he would have brought no more than two hundred dhirhams, a moderate price, in the slave market. They also spread stories that Frederick was not much of a Christian because of his sincere interest in Islam—stories that were picked up by Christian churchmen and later used by the Curia against Frederick. But it is clear that Frederick felt he was a loyal Christian; his treatment of heretics shows that he did not believe in deviation in Christian belief. However, his attitude

4. Masson, *Frederick II of Hohenstaufen*, 143.

toward the papacy and church leaders led to his being demonized by the bureaucracy of the church

Frederick remained in Jerusalem over a month. This, along with his time in Cyprus, was his major exposure to the East, and it had a substantial effect on him. He studied the structure of the Dome of the Rock closely, and it inspired one palace he built later. He had been given several falcons, and the services of Arabic falconers. Arabic falconers used hoods, which was unknown in Europe, and Frederick discussed hoods in his book on falconry and introduced their use to Europe. Also, prior Norman rulers of the Kingdom of Sicily had harems in their palace. Frederick saw that rulers in the Arab world brought their harems with them on their travels, and he adopted this practice on his return to Europe.

Now Frederick had to deal with the reactions of the Europeans in the crusader states. The patriarch of Jerusalem laid an interdict on his own city because of Frederick's presence at the Church of the Holy Sepulchre and his negotiating with Muslims. This meant no church services could be held in Jerusalem, to the dismay of the pilgrims. There was also the matter of the lands now secured from the Muslims. Much of it had previously been in the hands of the church, but Frederick awarded the land to nobles of proven loyalty, mostly Teutonic knights. The church formally protested this action, but Frederick dismissed the protest.

Frederick also faced problems in his relationships with the merchants of Acre and Damascus. Most of the merchants in Acre were Italian, and they worried that Frederick would impose Sicilian-like conditions for operating in the Kingdom of Jerusalem. Damascus merchants were the main source of luxury goods for Europeans. These merchants were under siege, and they were very disappointed in the taking of Jerusalem.

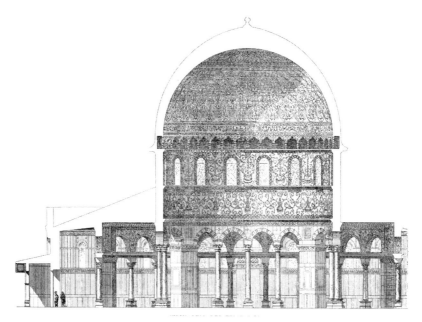

The Dome of the Rock in Jerusalem, a sacred place for Muslims, protected by
Frederick II per his agreement with al-Kamil. (*Kirchliche Baukunst des
Abendlandes*)

Finally, the normal disputes of the resident nobility were
being referred to Frederick, who tried not to get caught up in
them. However, his judgment always led to someone's dissatis-
faction.

After Easter, Frederick was ready to leave. The papal expedition against the Kingdom of Sicily had been proceeding, and
the pope had spread the word that Frederick had died in the
Holy Land. Frederick felt he had fulfilled his vows and was
eager to return home. He left Jerusalem and headed to Acre,
where there was street fighting between factions that supported
and opposed him. Frederick surrounded the town with his
troops and pacified it. When he tried to slip out of town early
on May 1, 1229, he was spotted as he walked to his ship

docked at a pier in the butcher's quarter. The butchers of Acre displayed their displeasure with him by pelting his party with offal. John of Ibelin had followed Frederick to see him off, and he was able to disperse the mob.

Frederick next went to Tyre and named his representatives to govern in his absence. Frederick returned to Cyprus, where, during his absence, the enemies of the Ibelins had taken control. Frederick confirmed them in power and forbade John of Ibelin from returning to Cyprus. Frederick was able to secure some money to help him fund his crusading expenses. Frederick left Cyprus for the Kingdom of Sicily, arriving at Brindisi on June 10, 1229. He had been gone from the Kingdom of Sicily slightly less than a year.

Frederick's crusade was unique in the context of the other crusades. There was very little bloodshed. The negotiations with the Muslims resulted in a restored Christian Kingdom of Jerusalem. The truce between the Kingdom of Jerusalem and al-Kamil held for the term agreed on in the treaty. Hence, the avowed goal of the crusade was met.

Frederick's dealings with the resident nobility of the crusader states in both Cyprus and the Kingdom of Jerusalem had been inept. The agents he left behind in the kingdom were caught up in disputes of the nobles for the entire ten years of the truce. His newly confirmed rulers of Cyprus were defeated by John of Ibelin, who reinstated Henry Lusignan on the throne. His family ruled Cyprus until the fifteenth century. Even though Cyprus continued to acknowledge that the emperor was overlord, Frederick and his successors had no influence there.

SIX

Return to Sicily

FREDERICK RETURNED to a kingdom in disorder. Pope Gregory IX had taken advantage of the emperor's absence to try to destroy his power using an intense propaganda campaign against Frederick, and by freeing Frederick's subjects from their oaths of allegiance to him. This attracted some interest in Lombardy, virtually none in Germany, and not much in Sicily.

Gregory also demanded tithes from the church in England, France, and Scandinavia to fund what he considered a just war against Frederick. All this activity was just short of a crusade. There was precedent for such a crusade against Christians: an ongoing campaign against heretics in southern France, declared by Pope Innocent III. Pope Gregory chose not to take this final step, particularly after Frederick had left on his own crusade. But John of Brienne was at the pope's side, and willing to lead papal forces into the Kingdom of Sicily. These troops were on a semicrusade, not using the crusader cross but the papal insignia of the Keys of St. Peter. Most of the participants were mercenaries, recruited mostly from French- or Spanish-speaking areas. They were interested in earthly rewards only.

John led this army against Frederick's lieutenant, Rainald of Spoleto. Rainald had claimed some land in the Papal States, and the pope was determined to throw him out. John's expedition succeeded, and Rainald was expelled in the winter of 1228-29. In early 1229, another papal army marched into the kingdom and met Sicilian resistance led by Henry de Morra, chief justiciar of the kingdom. The papal forces won a victory against Henry in March 1229, appearing to put the kingdom in jeopardy. Pope Gregory had made clear to his associates that he was not awarding sovereignty of the kingdom to any of them. Gregory was going to take over direct rule of the kingdom. He offered generous privileges to towns such as Naples, Gaeta, and Capua, on the model of the Lombard communes. News of the pope's advance reached the remaining Muslim areas of Sicily and led to resumption of guerrilla war there. The Muslims had not been happy with Frederick's treatment, but they had no desire to see how the pope would treat them. John of Brienne led his force, slowly, into Apulia, where the pope had promised John substantial lands.

As in Germany in 1212, and in the Kingdom in Sicily in 1220, Frederick's presence had a profound impact on this conflict. After he landed in Brindisi, he issued an appeal to the people of the kingdom to join him in expelling the invader. Many of the crusaders who were on their way back home were persuaded to aid him. Frederick led his forces to the northern border of the kingdom, where Capua was under siege. The papal forces mostly dissolved. Many of these troops had believed the pope when he claimed that Frederick was dead. Frederick tried to capture the forces of John of Brienne, but they retreated to the papal territories before he could catch them.

Frederick recaptured some towns that had welcomed the papal armies, including Cassino, San Germano, and Sora. In Frederick's view, these towns had been in rebellion against his rule. He decided to make an example of Sora by having it razed and many of its inhabitants killed. This was to impress upon other towns in the kingdom what would happen if they continued to oppose Frederick. This cruel policy worked. All the other towns that had been in rebellion, such as Foggio, Casal Nova, and Santo Severo, surrendered. Frederick punished these towns by tearing down their protective walls.

Frederick stopped his troops at the border of the kingdom. He did not wish to go further, which would have taken him into the Papal States. Frederick's fondest wish was to make peace with the pope. He chose to do it through diplomacy. His trusted associate Hermann von Salza led a delegation to see Gregory. Frederick's goal was to resume the relationship with the papacy that he had enjoyed during the reign of Honorius III. By July 1230, an agreement was reached. Gregory was not enthusiastic about it, but he had been pressured by cardinals who supported Frederick. The church's precarious financial situation played a role as well.

Frederick offered good terms, and Gregory accepted them in the agreements of San German and Ceprano. Frederick renounced his claims to legal authority against the church within the kingdom and promised to return lands to the Templars and Hospitallers that had been seized after his return from the Holy Land. In exchange, Frederick's excommunication was withdrawn. This was all confirmed in writing, and the final act was a dinner at Anagni. Frederick and Hermann von Salza joined the pope. No one knows what was said, but papal letters about Frederick became much more friendly. Frederick had again shown himself a master of diplomacy. Now he could turn his attention to the state of the kingdom.

FREDERICK AS LAWMAKER

Frederick had stated that the Kingdom of Sicily was the favorite of his realms. He had started organizing it during his residence as king from 1220 through 1228, but the dispute with the pope and planning for the crusade kept interfering. Now he took the opportunity to put his plans into effect.

Apart from two trips to northern Italy to deal with matters in Germany and Lombardy (which will be discussed later), Frederick spent the next five years in the kingdom. This was rare, because kings and emperors during this time led a peripatetic existence, traveling around and holding court throughout their domains. As Frederick's realms were the largest in Europe, he traveled more than anyone else. So his extended period in the kingdom is the closest he came to settling in one area.

His first concern was to codify legal practices in the kingdom. This was done at a meeting with the nobility at Melfi. Frederick issued the Constitutions of Melfi, also known as the *Liber Augustalis*, which went into effect in the summer of 1231. Frederick had commissioned an investigation of the legal practices of the kingdom after the conclusion of his peace with the pope. The investigation was too brief to allow innovation, but it did encourage the codification of old and proven laws. Frederick stressed that he was legislating as emperor, even though the laws applied only to the Kingdom of Sicily. The preservation of the Roman Catholic Church is mentioned before anything else, to address the criticism that he was an enemy of the church. The introduction to the constitutions stressed that Frederick's power was direct from God, with no intermediary. He claimed no need for the blessing of the pope for his rule. This was the philosophical basis for the continuing conflict with the papacy for the rest of Frederick's life.

Historians have different opinions on the significance of the Constitutions of Melfi. T.C. Van Cleve calls it "a remarkable document, revealing the genius of Frederick II."[1] David Abulafia states that "such an interpretation is based on wishful thinking . . . his legislation does not mark the coming of a new Justinian."[2] And Georgina Masson calls it the "Constitution of the Bureaucracy."[3]

It seems clear that Norman law was the basis for the entire project, but Norman law had never been used exclusively in the kingdom. As they had done in England, the Normans used the existing laws of the Kingdom of Sicily as well as their own traditions. The constitutions discussed Byzantine, Lombard, canon, and Norman legal practice, and Frederick used all of this background to make laws.

One statement in the constitutions stands out as quite different from the trend of the times. The special privileges of Normans (or Franks) in court were abolished with this ruling:

> We desire to end the ambiguity about a certain special right, or as it might more appropriately be termed, denial of right, practiced by the Franks and observed in civil and criminal cases until now. Thus we desire that all our subjects should know, under the terms of this law, that we, who weigh on our scales each individual's

1. Van Cleve, *The Emperor Frederick II*, 242.

2. Abulafia, *Frederick II: A Medieval Emperor*, 202.

3. Masson, *Frederick II of Hohenstaufen*, 159.

right to justice, insist that no distinction shall be made between persons in the judgment of the courts: justice is to be administered with equal force for each person, be he a Frank, a Roman, or a Lombard, be he plaintiff or defendant.[4]

Another law took this concept much further, allowing Jews and Muslims to initiate suits. It is noteworthy that this law was not based on the fact (which other legislation would confirm) that Jews and Muslims were "serfs of the chamber," but it was based on moral grounds. The legal treatment of Jews and Muslims was distinct from their religious treatment. Jews and Muslims were separated from the Christian community, but they did have specified rights. This was uncommon for the time.

A major part of the constitutions dealt with heresy. Judaism and Islam were not treated as heresy, but different religions subject to regulation. Christian heresy was condemned as treason. Here Frederick was not subordinate to the pope; he acted as a ruler subject only to divine authority. Because he had agreed at San Germano to respect ecclesiastical law, the sections of the constitutions dealing with the clergy made them subject to ecclesiastical law, avoiding the dispute that had torn apart Henry II and Thomas Becket in England in the twelfth century. Frederick was not picking any new fights with the church at this time.

The constitutions also laid out the secular justice system in the Kingdom of Sicily. The emperor made all appointments, and terms of office were for one year only, which was renewable. There was a grand master justiciar, who presided over the High Court. There were two master justiciars, one handling the

4. Abulafia, *Frederick II: A Medieval Emperor*, 209.

mainland portion of the kingdom, another the island of Sicily. And there were regular justiciars, who were the governors of the nine provinces that made up the kingdom. The regular justiciars were answerable to their superior officers and to the emperor. The justiciars could not be natives of the provinces they administered, and their families were prohibited from settling in those provinces. A justiciar mostly concerned himself with criminal cases, but civil appeals were in his jurisdiction, and he was required to proclaim tax requirements.

The justiciars had substantial staffs to assist them. There were judges, legal counselors, notaries, and clerks, all paid by the emperor. All of these officers were subject to being called on by the emperor to provide personal services as well, such as helping him in his hunting, or in his natural-science inquiries. They were all expected to act as a check upon each other, and subjects in their areas had the right to present complaints against them twice yearly.

Frederick had announced the constitutions at a meeting of the ecclesiastical leaders and the nobility at Melfi in 1231. There had been small uprisings in 1231 against the authority of the emperor in Messina and other parts of the island. Frederick went to investigate and determined that some form of contact with the nonnoble population was necessary. A decree was issued in Messina in 1233 that there would be twice yearly meetings in each province. An imperial representative would be present, and the entire population was eligible to attend. This representative had to submit a written report to Frederick. Masson uses the phrase "calling of the Third Estate" to describe these meetings.[5] That view seems excessive, because there was no legislative intent, such as the meetings of the Third

5. Masson, *Frederick II of Hohenstaufen*, 171.

Estate in France. These were meetings to inform the people of the emperor's will, and to hear grievances. These meetings took place throughout the rest of Frederick's reign.

With the announcement of the constitutions, Frederick was proclaiming himself as the embodiment of law, coming from God. His absolute superiority in this area did not mean the end of the feudal system in the kingdom, however. There was no question of destroying feudalism entirely, but the fiefs, heirs, and obligations of military service were put under the control of the emperor. He had already assumed similar power in 1221, when he reviewed all land titles in the kingdom. He was continuing to control the holders of those titles. The fact that a small number of barons was unhappy with this was not important to Frederick. Later in his reign, these barons would be contacted by the pope and asked to rebel.

At this time, rulers felt it was their supreme duty to dispense justice and keep the peace. Frederick's justice system has been detailed above. The peace was kept by the military and a secret police. Frederick had a marshal of the kingdom as the head of the army and an admiral as the head of the fleet. As he got older, Frederick became more suspicious of his subjects, and it appears that sometime during his stay in the kingdom from 1230 through 1235, he organized a secret police. There are no records extant of the operation of this department, but it becomes clear later in his reign that Frederick was well-informed of possible conspiracies and possible opponents in the realm.

MATTERS OF FINANCE

In any realm, finance is what allows the ruler to take the actions he wants to take. As emperor, Frederick ruled over a vast area of Europe north of the Papal States, but he did not realize any money from those areas except in special circumstances. He needed to be present, particularly in Germany, to raise money. If he was not, the imperial income was spent by local officials in the area it was raised. The same was true in Lombardy, with the added problem that collection of any imperial income was always contested, and required an imperial army to be present, which added vastly to the expense of the collection. When he needed money, Frederick tended to secure it in the Kingdom of Sicily. The kingdom had been known as the richest in Europe under Roger II and the two Williams. Frederick had started the process of restoring that status, and he now turned his full attention to the matter.

There was no theory of economic growth in medieval times. The rulers usually tried to encourage trade, but under their own control. There was a growing merchant class in northern Italy, but it had no counterpart in the kingdom. The merchants there tended to be citizens of other realms, particularly from Pisa on the island of Sicily, and from Venice on the Adriatic coast of the mainland. Frederick had ejected the Genoese from the kingdom. He tried to control the trade of the kingdom, and his methods, determined through trial and error, yielded mixed results.

Identical with all extensive domains in Europe, the main occupation and industry in the kingdom was agriculture. The island of Sicily had been a major granary of the Roman Empire, and it continued to produce a surplus of grain for sale overseas. This was also true of parts of the mainland kingdom, particularly the plains of Apulia. Frederick was the largest landowner in the kingdom. The other landowners had to ship their grain to state warehouses for export and pay a royal export tax on it. The king was exempt from this tax, which was quite a nice little advantage. This was also true for the second most important crop in the kingdom, wool.

Frederick tried to encourage agricultural production. Silkworks had been established under Roger II, and Frederick tried to expand them. He eventually handed over this industry to the Jews of Trani. He offered vacant lands in Apulia and Sicily to Ghibelline exiles from northern Italy. He assisted the Muslims in the area of Lucera by giving them lands and plough teams. He brought Jews from North Africa to grow dates and indigo in western Sicily. Frederick also admired the Cistercian order of monks, who had a reputation as the best farmers of Europe. He often observed their practices, mostly when in northern Italy, and tried to export them to the kingdom. To a great extent, Frederick abolished the existing internal tolls within the kingdom.

State warehouses existed in every port in the kingdom as part of the system for collecting import taxes. In Giovanni Boccaccio's *Decameron*, there is a description of how the system worked in the fourteenth century under the successors to the Hohenstaufen:

> There was, and perhaps still is, a custom in all maritime countries that have ports, that all merchants arriving there with merchandise, should, on discharging, bring all their goods into a warehouse, called in many places a dogana, and maintained by the state, . . . where those that are assigned to that office allot to each merchant, on receipt of an invoice for all his goods and the value thereof, a room in which he stored his goods under lock and key; whereupon the said officers of the dogana enter all the merchant's goods to his credit in the book of the dogana, and afterwards make him pay duty thereon, or on such part as he withdraws from the warehouse.[6]

6. Abulafia, *Frederick II: A Medieval Emperor*, 216.

This was the administrative means of securing import tax on trade in the kingdom. The ports were much more important to the kingdom than trade across land borders, which was only with the Papal States. The papal domain was not very active in trade, and trade was much easier by sea than by land in this era.

The Kingdom of Sicily's geographical position put it in the middle of the trade system of the Mediterranean. However, at this time most of the carrying trade was in the hands of Venice, Pisa, and Genoa. They controlled the luxury trade that was conducted through the Near East. They also did most of the bulk trade of grain and wool. Frederick tried to influence these parties by granting privileges in the empire, but not the kingdom. He had booted the Genoese out of the kingdom, and never granted them special privileges. All these parties were allowed to trade in the kingdom, but under the control of the tax administrators. At this time, the Venetians controlled one of the great sources of trade and wealth in the world, Constantinople, which they had conquered in 1204. The Venetians wanted to deal with the kingdom but had no pressing need to do so. Frederick continued to treat the Pisans better, as they had been and remained consistent allies of his.

The Constitutions of Melfi had proclaimed state monopoly on salt, iron, dyeing of cloth, and hemp. Hemp was used in the navy from sources that were being built up in the kingdom. Dyeing was turned over to the Jews of Capua and Naples. Iron had many military uses, and so was controlled by the state. The price of salt and iron were fixed by the state, and sale was controlled by four men in the royal service. These monopolies were continued by subsequent regimes that took over the kingdom, and the monopoly on salt continued into the early nineteenth century.

Trade and taxes required a sound currency. The kingdom
was dealing with two types of metal money. In the Near East
and North Africa, gold was the basis of currency. In the northern realms of the empire, and northern Europe in general, silver was the basis. Frederick decided to issue coins of both gold
and silver. In 1231, the mint at Messina issued a new gold coin,
the augustale, which showed Frederick's pretension at being
universal as well as local monarch. The inscription on the coin
proclaims his status as emperor, even though the coin was
issued by the Kingdom of Sicily. One side shows the abbrevia-
tion "*Cesave Improm*," which stands for "*Cesar Augustus
Imperator Romanorum*," and the reverse says "*Fridericus*."
The coin was of exceptional purity, 20.5 karats of gold. It
appears that the main source of gold was tribute payments
from North Africa. The gold coinage was mostly used for royal
purposes and did not usually achieve wide circulation. This
coin proved so effective as a sound currency that it was minted
through the end of the reign of Frederick's son Manfred in
1266.

Production of the more common currency, silver coin, was
centralized by closing one mint and concentrating production
at Brindisi. A sufficient supply of silver came from trade with
northern Italian cities, and Frederick had access to silver from
German sources. The silver denarius was minted starting in
1225, and was the basic currency of the realm. This is what was
paid to the state for taxes. Frederick tried to impose a fixed
exchange rate between the gold and silver currencies, but it is
not clear if he succeeded.

Because Frederick held the kingdom as a personal possession
and was the largest landowner in the realm, his personal
finances were mixed up with the government accounts. There is
evidence that he took advantage of situations to make a larger

Coins issued by Frederick II. This is the angustale, a gold coin issued by the Kingdom of Sicily. (*Art of Falconry [1943]*)

personal profit. In 1239, he heard that Genoese traders had learned of a famine in North Africa and were buying up stocks of Sicilian grain to sell there. Frederick ordered Sicilian ports closed, then negotiated with the government of Tunis in North Africa to sell it a large amount of wheat at a substantial profit. Most of the wheat was from his lands, and he collected export tax on the wheat not from his lands.

Even with import/export taxes and direct trade providing income, there was not enough for the military expenses incurred by the protracted dispute with the papacy and Lombard cities. Hence, another source of tax revenue was implemented: the *Collecta*, a levy on land owned by anyone other than the king. Originally intended to be imposed only in times of great financial stringency, the *Collecta* eventually became an annual tax, and in 1248 the total collected was one hundred thirty thousand ounces of gold.

The administration of collection of the import/export taxes and the *Collecta* was in the hands of the master chamberlain. This official had been in charge of tax collection and also the royal lands, but the duties on the royal lands were given to another official to allow the master chamberlain to concentrate on public finances. Frederick had only two master chamber-lains in his reign in the kingdom. The first was named Richard, a Sicilian thought to be of Muslim stock, who may have been a eunuch. A year after Richard died, Frederick appointed Giovanni il Moro master chamberlain. He was a Muslim, thought to be the son of a Muslim slave and black woman. He lived in Lucera and was in charge of the harem as well.

The taxes to be secured under the *Collecta* were pronounced by the justiciars of each province on a yearly basis, on instruc-tions from the emperor. Collecting these taxes was the job of *bajuli*, who were responsible to the master chamberlain. *Bajuli* were the most numerous officials in the kingdom; there were about two thousand in the province of Abruzzi alone. The *bajuli* worked with the subordinate justice officials to collect the taxes, and they appear to have done a good job of it. Frederick was able to keep up his struggle with the pope and the Lombard communes mostly with money from the kingdom. He borrowed some money from the emerging banks of Rome and Lombardy, and was always careful to pay them back quick-ly in order to retain his credit.

The Kingdom of Sicily was considered the richest in Europe from the time of Roger II through the reign of Frederick. After Frederick's death, Pope Clement IV, who invited Charles of Anjou to conquer the kingdom, said in a letter to Charles, "It is strange that you should complain of the poverty of a Realm (the Kingdom of Sicily) from which that noble man Frederick, in spite of his having incurred greater expenses than your own, enriched enormously both himself and his family and satisfied as well Lombardy, Tuscany, the March of Ancona, the Trevisan March and Germany."[7] Clement still considered the kingdom

7. Masson, *Frederick II of Hohenstaufen*, 165.

to be a rich state. However, the exactions of Frederick started the transition of this area from one of the richest in Europe to one of the poorest.

theorique come de celles qui re
gardent la pratique. Les au
tres parties de lespecial confide
racion sont de celles meismes

sonner selonc les gouuernemes
des choses dou monde par lus
de cest art entremetront a la
fois totes a lor aures-li pour

Frederick II receiving falcons. Falconry was a consuming, life-long interest of Frederick. (*Art of Falconry [1943]*)

SEVEN

Personality, Family, and Interests

FREDERICK II HAD A UNIQUE REPUTATION for his personality and cultural activities. Contemporary observers called him *Stupor Mundi* ("Wonder of the World") and *Immutator Mundi* ("Transformer of the World"). These observers were usually churchmen, who were the most literate class in Europe at the time, and their experiences were quite different from Frederick's. This led the churchmen to stress the unusual aspects of Frederick's personality. It is clear from all sources that Frederick was different personally from the norm, even for monarchs.

Frederick was both emperor of the Holy Roman Empire and king of Sicily, which gave him a separate status from the rest of humanity. Except for the episode in the town of Constance in 1212, when he persuaded its citizens to help him against Otto, there are no stories in the sources I have read showing that Frederick had a common touch with the nonaristocrats in his realms. His personal dealings were with fellow aristocrats, clergy, court officials, and diplomats, and those parties left many accounts of his character. The emperor always expected to be treated as a ruler in any official matter, and people who did not honor this status were punished if possible. In fact, the entire Lombard conflict may have been an attempt to enforce this point.

Once his official status was made clear, it appears that Frederick could deal with members of the court, selected scholars, or visiting dignitaries on a friendly, personal basis. All contemporary accounts cited in my sources stress his charm. This was exhibited over a large swath of Europe, because of the itinerant nature of his court. If someone piqued the emperor's intellectual interest, that person was brought to court to meet Frederick, or a correspondence was initiated. Many instances of this are cited in the sources.

Frederick's family was constantly changing after Constance died in 1222. As noted earlier, it appears his marriage to Constance was his most successful. She was ten years older than Frederick, and was his only wife who was crowned empress. She was also made regent of the Kingdom of Sicily when Frederick went to Germany in 1212. He showed real sorrow at her death, and always respected her memory. There was one child from that union, Henry. Henry had virtually no relationship with his father, like Frederick's own experience in childhood. In Frederick's case, that was due to the death of his father. In Henry's case, Frederick left Sicily for Germany soon after Henry's birth, and they were separated for four years. Then Constance and Henry were summoned to Germany, and they remained with Frederick for four more years. Finally, Henry was left in Germany in 1220, in the care of guardians, and his parents returned to the Kingdom of Sicily. The consequence of all this was a strained relationship between Frederick and his eldest legitimate son.

Like his marriage to Constance, Frederick's other marriages were political, arranged without his ever having met the bride prior to the ceremony. His treatment of Isabella of Jerusalem was resented by her family, and stories of mistreatment were spread throughout the church and used against Frederick. Frederick had already had some illegitimate children by the time of his marriage to Isabella, and they were raised at his court. Only one of the mothers is known, but they all seem to have been ladies of the court. Soon after his trip to the Holy Land and after experiencing firsthand the treatment of women by Muslims, Frederick adopted their practices. He recruited dancing girls from the Muslim enclave of Lucera. He continually stated that these women were just performers, but no one believed him. Frederick kept a harem after his experiences in the Near East. This harem was based in Lucera, but he took some women with him on his expeditions to Germany and northern Italy. This practice was cited in many papal documents condemning Frederick. It is not known how many children resulted from this harem, or if any of his acknowledged children came from there. He expected his later wife, Isabella of England, to spend time in the harem, which must have been a shock for her.

The sources indicate that Frederick had three other legitimate children besides Henry. Frederick's son by Isabella of Jerusalem, Conrad, became Frederick's successor to the thrones of the empire and the Kingdom of Sicily. At the death of his mother, Conrad became king of Jerusalem. He was raised in the court of the Kingdom of Sicily. Frederick's final legitimate son, by Isabella of England, was also named Henry. He died in 1253, at age fifteen. Frederick's only legitimate daughter,

Margaret, was married off to the margrave of Meissen, an ally of Frederick's in Germany.

Frederick had eleven acknowledged illegitimate children. The only mother of these children who is known is Bianca Lancia, the mother of Manfred and Constance. She was probably representative of the type of woman who was involved with Frederick without being married to him. Her family was a noble one from Piedmont who had long supported the Hohenstaufen. Frederick had met her brother Manfred on his initial trip to Germany in 1212, and Manfred Lancia acted on the emperor's behalf in northern Italy in the early 1220s. Eventually, the whole family moved to the Kingdom of Sicily, and Manfred was listed in court documents as an officer of the highest rank in that realm from 1231 through 1234. At some point, Frederick met Bianca, and their son Manfred was born in 1232. Georgina Masson states that after the death of Isabella of England, Frederick and Bianca were married secretly.[1] Bianca was certainly endowed with lands in the kingdom, which she left to her son Manfred. These lands eventually became part of the dower of the queens of Sicily, given to each new queen at the time of her marriage.

Frederick was known as an affectionate and demanding father to all his children after his eldest. It appears Manfred was his favorite. Manfred was certainly initiated into Frederick's favorite sport of falconry. It was due to Manfred's request that Frederick wrote his book on falconry, and Manfred was responsible for the book's survival. The male children were given responsibility at a young age. Enzio was made king of Sardinia and was a major military leader during Frederick's campaigns in northern Italy. Another son, Frederick, was sent

1. Masson, *Frederick II of Hohenstaufen*, 213.

to the Holy Land as his father's representative and became known as Frederick of Antioch. Richard of Theate was vicar-general of Romagna, Spoleto, and the Marches from 1247 until he died in 1249. Manfred eventually succeeded his half-brother Conrad as ruler of the Kingdom of Sicily and was Frederick's last male descendent to rule.

Frederick's daughters were used as royal children were used throughout Europe at this time: to cement or create new family alliances. Two, Margaret and Violante, were married to members of the Aquino family of the kingdom to retain their loyalty. Besides being a prominent family of supporters, it was also the family that produced the most famous graduate of the University of Naples, St. Thomas Aquinas. Catherine was married to the marquis of Caretto, whose lands bordered on Genoa. Manfred's full sister, Constance, was married to the pretender to the throne of the Byzantine Empire, John Vatatzes.

Although Frederick did insist on being treated in a way befitting his status at court, the sources state, many people showed him undue deference at times. Frederick appears to have tolerated this, but he preferred the private company of those whom he could treat as intellectual equals. Frederick's oldest political and religious ally was Archbishop Berard of Palermo, who had been with Frederick since before he took over the kingdom. Another close associate, who had Frederick's entire trust, was Hermann von Salza. Frederick often used both of these men for diplomatic missions, and they never disappointed him.

Like Berard and Herman, medieval statesmen serving someone of Frederick's rank were usually churchmen or nobles. But another prominent close associate of Frederick's broke that mold. Piero della Vigna had been brought to Frederick's attention by Berard. Piero was from a nonnoble family, and he never took holy orders. He was from Capua, in the kingdom. Capua was known for its school of *ars dictandi*, the formal style of Latin writing most used during this period. Piero learned this writing method while young, then studied law at the university in Bologna. After he started in Frederick's service, he distinguished himself enough to be put in charge of the project that resulted in the Constitutions of Melfi. He is the only person other than Frederick mentioned in that document.

By 1235, Piero had been named *logothete* for the emperor, and he was trusted with sensitive diplomatic missions like Berard and Hermann. The main job of the *logothete* was to act as mouthpiece for the emperor, which Piero did in writing and speaking. At times when policy was pronounced by the emperor, Piero did the actual speaking, in Latin, with Frederick looking on from his throne. Piero was also in charge of Frederick's political correspondence, and he engaged in continual sniping with the papal Curia. Piero della Vigna was an example of how high a civil servant could rise in the medieval world, and his fall was equally spectacular, as we will see later.

By this time Frederick was forty years old and in generally good health. He is described as being below middle height (estimated in the various sources as around five feet six inches) and having a sturdy build. He was thought of as charming by people in his circle, and was obviously very successful with women. He was known as a fine horseman, and was well-practiced in the use of arms. While being a ruler was his main vocation in life, Frederick had intellectual and physical interests that were important to him.

PATRON OF THE ARTS AND ARCHITECTURE

Frederick received a rich intellectual inheritance in the Kingdom of Sicily. The court of Roger II was known as the leading intellectual center in Europe during the twelfth century.

It was a meeting place of Greek, Muslim, and Jewish scholars, and Roger encouraged this activity. After Roger's death, the tolerance for this multicultural exchange decreased. William I started the process of Latinizing the court, and it was continued by William II. During Frederick's minority, the instability of the kingdom led to the continued departure of leading scholars. The main gathering point after this was in Toledo in Spain, which became the leading multicultural scholastic center of Europe. The products of the Toledo translations, such as works by Aristotle, Ptolemy, and Plato, spread slowly throughout Europe, including the empire and the kingdom.

Some Jewish translators of ancient works secured from the Muslim world remained in the kingdom, and they were at Frederick's court. These translators were not Italians, but had come from Provence. Their work continued during Frederick's reign. They translated the commentaries of Averroes on Aristotle, and also the *Almagest* of Ptolemy, the most complete book on ancient astronomy. Another book translated at the Sicilian court was by one of the leading thinkers of the time, the Jewish physician Moses ben Maimon, also known as Maimonides or Rambam. His work *Guide for the Perplexed* was translated from the Hebrew in Sicily in the late twelfth century. The translation spread around the kingdom and was read by Thomas Aquinas during his time there. Frederick allowed the Jews at court to continue at their translating and intellectual pursuits, met and had discussions with visiting Jewish scholars, and also imported Jews to spread their agricultural knowledge into the kingdom. But he did not bring more Jews into the court, letting the trend toward larger numbers of Latin personnel at court continue. Frederick was much more tolerant than other Western leaders, but he did not turn back the preference for less Jewish participation at the court. Compared to the attitude of other leaders of western Europe, such as Louis IX of France and the various popes, Frederick was very enlightened.

The two other ethnic groups that had been prominent at Roger's court, Arabic and Greek, were not prominent at Frederick's. Frederick continued to correspond with Muslim rulers and wise men. He continued his contact with al-Kamil, and exchanged gifts with him. There was a diplomatic tradition at this time in Muslim circles of sending intellectual questions to prominent scholars in other realms. Frederick played this game with vigor, the only Christian monarch known to have participated. He sent these questions to learned men in Ceuta, Damascus, and Yemen. His intermediary with these Muslim scholars was his court philosopher, Master Theodore, who was thought to be a Christian from Antioch. The Muslim enclave at Lucera was a favorite spot of Frederick's, but not for intellectual pursuits. Muslims from there were used as soldiers, and they became a very loyal royal bodyguard.

Frederick appears to have had little contact with the Greeks in his kingdom. Some court documents were issued in Greek, but no real intellectual activity was conducted in it. This was true even though there was still a strong Greek community in southern Italy, and the Orthodox Church continued to operate in the kingdom.

The kingdom was a center for poetry in the early thirteenth century. This poetry was derivative of the Provençal poets who had made courtly love the main subject for lyric poetry in the twelfth century. Provençal poets had composed in the vernacular, and Frederick had firsthand contact with the similar German *minnesingers* on his trip to Germany. The sources are clear that these poets used whatever dialect they were familiar with, and the poems have come down to us in Tuscanized forms. Tuscan became the Italian literary language, following the towering example of Dante, in the fourteenth century. Dante cited Sicilian poetry as a type he was trying to improve on in the *Divine Comedy*.

Several poets whose names are known from this time also held some kind of office under Frederick and his successors. At this time, there was no way for a poet to make a living off just his writing. The poets whose works have been remembered were all associated with a court in some way, or were nobles themselves. For example, Giacomo da Lentini was entrusted with the care of some castles in south Italy. And Ruggero de Amicus was sent to Egypt as ambassador in 1241 (and was involved in a conspiracy against Frederick in 1246). The most versatile appears to have been Jacopo Mostacci, who was falconer for Frederick, then jurist for Manfred and succeeding rulers. These artists needed multiple occupations because Frederick's court was itinerant, and he did not take poets with him on his travels.

The priciple theme of these poets was the popular one at the time, courtly love. The subject of such poetry was a woman, presumably married to someone else. We generally assume that these poems were of longing only. The patron of the original Provençal poets, Duke William of Aquitaine, did produce some lines in that vein, but he also wrote more graphically about what would happen when he conquered the woman. Frederick is thought to have composed several poems of courtly love, but their true authorship is in dispute. His illegitimate sons Manfred and Enzio did produce such works. These are more poignant for Enzio, for reasons that will be discussed later. Manfred and Enzio would have picked up this taste at court because they traveled with the emperor, unlike Frederick's other children.

Little evidence remains of Frederick's patronage of, or taste in, painting or sculpture. No paintings have survived from his court. The primary form of physical representation in the king-dom in Roger's time was mosaics. Many of those survive in churches in the kingdom. Roger seems to have commissioned mosaics to be in competition with Constantinople. That com-petition did not exist for Frederick, as he did not initiate any religious works. Some repair work was done on existing mosaics, but Frederick did not commission any new ones. One reason is that these mosaics were in churches, and Frederick was not a church builder.

Evidence of Frederick's patronage of sculpture comes from one building. The Gate of Capua was built in Frederick's reign, then torn down by the Spanish in 1557. The sculptures from this building still exist. They are a figure of Justice, a seated emperor (now headless), and two large busts of judges. These figures, which appeared at a mainland entrance to the king-dom, represented the justice that was enforced in the kingdom. The figures show an attempt to copy Roman style. This was another way for Frederick to show that he was the universal monarch, like the Roman emperors of antiquity. The Gate of Capua was started in 1234, when Frederick still had some financial reserves. When these reserves were used up, Frederick sharply reduced his spending on art and architecture.

One artist who appears to have benefited from Frederick's patronage of sculpture was Nicola Pisano, a native of Apulia. He seems to have been trained in one of the sculpture studios active at Frederick's court, and he may have participated in cre-ating the figures for the Gate of Capua. After Frederick died, Nicola migrated to Pisa. He founded a studio there and creat-ed a well-known Adoration of the Magi as part of the pulpit of the Pisa Baptistry. One of the students in his studio was his son, Giovanni Pisano, who also became a well-known sculptor in Tuscany. Giovanni's best-known work exhibited a knowledge

Sculptures of two judges that once decorated the Gate of Capua. The one on the right is thought to be Piero della Vigna. (*Van Cleve*)

of Greek and Roman sculpture that probably came from Frederick's activities in seeking out ancient sculptures.

Buildings are the main surviving evidence of Frederick's patronage. Frederick called his castles "places of solace."[2] He improved old castles and built new ones throughout the kingdom. The Norman castle, a creation of the Norman expansion in Europe in the eleventh and twelfth centuries, was the most important secular building style in Europe at that time. Norman castles abounded in the kingdom as a result of the rise to power of the Hauteville family and because of the tendency of Norman nobles to build castles on land they claimed. Most of the castles were in disrepair, so Frederick took those over and restored the most important ones. One example of this was in Bari, where an old Byzantine fortress that had been used by Norman lords was restored. Frederick built up other fortresses

2. Masson, *Frederick II of Hohenstaufen*, 173.

on the Apulian coast. In Apulia, he also built his palace in Lucera, surrounded by loyal Muslims. All that remains of this palace is its rectangular base.

Not long after Frederick issued the Constitutions of Melfi in 1231, some towns on the island of Sicily rose against them. The uprising was quickly put down, but Frederick decided to take a tour of Sicily and determine what needed to be done for security. He decided to build a series of castles on the island. Some were built on existing foundations, and some were new. The buildings were to be used for defense, and as a residence if the king was present. Frederick returned only once to the island after this visit, staying in Palermo, so these castles were not used as residences until after he died. Frederick had access to many castles in the kingdom, but none was the main focus of his court because of his constant movement.

One kind of building is conspicuously absent in Frederick's output: religious. This century was the time of the birth of the great cathedrals of northern Europe. This activity mostly took place in France and England, realms not even nominally ruled by Frederick. However, he was familiar with such activity in northern Italy and Germany. He never founded a new church nor funded any religious building. Frederick's correspondences about the church indicate his reasons: he believed that the church needed to go back to the poverty of its principles and avoid wealth and corruption. Frederick was known to be sympathetic with the aims of the Franciscan order, whose members took a vow of poverty. While Frederick was not averse to spending his wealth on buildings and art, he never did so for religious foundations.

The most studied, and best preserved, structure Frederick built was the Castel del Monte in Apulia. This was not a great castle, intended to be a residence, but a hunting lodge. Hunting

Castel del Monte in Apulia. This hunting lodge is the best-preserved building from Frederick's reign. (*Top, Andrewes; middle, Art of Falconry [1943]; bottom, Abulafia*)

was Frederick's great passion as a recreation. Frederick built the Castel del Monte in the last decade of his life, and it is not clear how often he was able to use it. It was built on a hill in open country. There were facilities for the keeping of falcons, and for the falconers. The building has many carvings, all of various kinds of birds. It is not large, and it is not luxurious. It was built at a time when Frederick faced other financial demands, but it shows how important hunting and falconry were to him.

FREDERICK AS SCIENTIST

Frederick was both a man of his times and ahead of his time. This is nowhere more true than in his scientific interests. His inquiries into the state of the universe were conducted fully in the context of his time. He used the language of his time, and the methods of his time, to reach conclusions that were based on what he read from past authorities, and what he could observe. Frederick's inquiries into the natural world were done by a different method. Even though they were guided by past authorities, he trusted nothing but his own eyes and experience. The result of this was a remarkable work, *De arte venandi cum avibus*, usually translated as *The Art of Falconry*. Both of these kinds of inquiries will be discussed below.

Frederick was thought of as a skeptic, or heretic, by the Catholic Church, particularly in his later days, and especially because he was continually asking questions about the universe. He was not content with the certainties of faith. He sent inquiries to Muslim authorities and explored them with scholars of his own court. The main person he consulted with at court was Michael Scot.

Michael Scot was a good example of the itinerant scholar of this era. He appears to have been born in Scotland in the 1170s. As a young man, he studied at Oxford and Paris. He was trained in philosophy and mathematics. He made his way to Toledo, then the leading center of translation of ancient scientific works. Michael was involved in the translation of several works, copies of which he had in his library. These works would have been translated from Arabic into Latin. It is clear Michael spoke those languages, and possibly Hebrew as well. He then made his way to the papal court, and stayed there for some time in the early 1220s. He must have taken holy orders somewhere along the way, because Pope Honorius III offered him a benefice in Ireland, which he turned down. In the mid-1220s, Michael made his way into Frederick's service as court philosopher and astrologer.

Michael appears to have also been the court magician. He had enough of a reputation for magic that his name came down all the way to early nineteenth century Scotland and was used by Walter Scott in the *Lay of the Last Minstrel*. Astrology and magic were not scorned by people interested in science in the thirteenth century, but were considered legitimate fields of study, even by the church. Frederick shared the prevailing belief that astrology could explain the workings of heaven on mankind. He believed enough to consult astrologers about when to consummate his second and third marriages to assure the birth of a son. In the case of his third marriage, he was told to wait one day after the ceremony, and he did.

Although Michael Scot was a scholar, he believed some of the contemporary "old wives' tales" and spread them as scientific facts. One was a method to determine the sex of an unborn child. One would ask the mother to extend a hand. If she extended her right hand, it would be a boy; her left hand, a girl.

Frederick asked Michael to answer the larger questions about the structure of the universe, which dealt with the place of heaven, purgatory, and hell. Frederick famously asked him to measure the distance from the top of a tower to heaven. Michael answered, and Frederick later had the tower lowered by a few feet. He then asked Michael to measure it again, and Michael was smart enough to answer that either heaven had moved up, or the tower had shrunk. Dante had heard enough of these types of stories about Michael Scot to put him in the eighth circle of hell, in the category of fortune tellers and diviners.

These abilities as a showman would have been necessary as a court astrologer, but they are not an indication that either Michael Scot or Frederick were not interested in the hard facts of science. It was known throughout the circle of people they dealt with that they enjoyed learning about the world around them. Many rulers used this fact when it came time to send Frederick gifts. He received many animals that were considered exotic in the Europe of his day, including elephants, cheetahs, camels, and others from Africa and the Middle East. These and more were gathered into a menagerie that traveled with Frederick. The menagerie astonished many in northern Italy and Germany in Frederick's later years. The ruler of Damascus sent Frederick a map of the universe in silver, which he was known to have valued highly (and which later was captured and melted down to make coins). In return for the map, Frederick sent a polar bear, probably from Iceland, which was unknown in Damascus and caused quite a stir.

Michael Scot served Frederick as court astrologer and philosopher, traveling with the court, until his death in 1236. His successor, Master Theodore, did not travel with the court. Theodore wrote a work on hygiene at Frederick's request. Frederick was known to take daily baths when possible, which was not common in Europe at the time.

When Frederick's travels took him to the neighborhoods of prominent scholars, he sought them out. One example was a visit Frederick made to Pisa in the early 1220s. He contacted Leonardo Fibonacci, a leading figure in mathematics who is credited with introducing Arabic numbers to Europe. He submitted several mathematical questions to Leonardo, who answered them to Frederick's satisfaction. Leonardo in 1225 dedicated his next book, *Liber Quadratorum*, to Frederick. Leonardo sent Frederick a revised edition of his work on arithmetic, *Liber Abaci*, in 1228, which was dedicated to Michael Scot. Due to the itinerant nature of Frederick's court, he made many such personal contacts.

Whether Frederick was traveling around his realms or staying in one place for awhile, one activity was always very important to him: hunting. This was a time before firearms, of course, and hunting with bow and arrow was as difficult as it had always been. The preferred way to hunt, if you could afford it, was with the help of animals, including horses and dogs. Frederick was known as a fine horseman, and he sponsored a stud in the kingdom to keep him supplied with good horses. He asked the person in charge of the stud farm, Giordano Ruffo, to write a tract on the care, diseases, and treatment of diseases of horses. He did, but it was not completed until after Frederick died. The volume, *De Medicina Equorum*, became a standard work used in Europe until the nineteenth century.

There were several options for hunting with animals. The ancient method cited in Greek and Roman sources was to use horses and dogs, and to make the kill with nets and spears. This was preferred for larger animals, such as boars and bears. Frederick's main method of hunting was with falcons, and falconry, the ancient practice of catching animals with trained birds of prey, was a consuming interest for him. It is not known how or when he was initiated into falconry, but by Frederick's time, it had become the sport of kings in Europe, the Middle

East, and parts of Asia. Frederick's entire court correspondence for the period 1239–40 still exists, and approximately one-third of his letters, written to officials in the kingdom while he was on military campaign in northern Italy, had to do with his falcons. The worst military defeat he suffered was because he took a day off while on campaign to go hunting with his falcons. Another, possibly apocryphal, comment shows what he thought of falconry. During this time, the Mongol Empire was making incursions into Europe. Before these expeditions, the Mongols sent communications to all rulers, asking them to submit. Frederick never had to deal with the Mongols because they were recalled due to the death of their khan before they reached Western Europe. However, he did get one of these communications, and he told his associates he would submit if he could serve as the khan's falconer.

Frederick's interest was intellectual as well as physical. One of Michael Scot's great assets was his possession, from his days in Toledo, of Aristotle's zoological treatise *De Animalibus* and a shorter, companion work by Avicenna. Frederick later had Master Theodore translate the current Arabic work on falconry, and then used his own knowledge of Arabic to correct and notate this work while waiting out one of his sieges in Lombardy. His absorption of this knowledge is on display in his own work, where he constantly refers to the Philosopher (Aristotle) and other authorities he had read.

But Frederick's main source of information about falconry, and birds in general, was through his own hunting experience. Because of his extensive travels, he was able to experience hunting in many kinds of environments. He was familiar with Arab practice from his trip to the Holy Land, for example. As his partiality to falconry became known to others, he was able to secure falcons from all over the parts of the world with which he was in contact——Africa, the Middle East, and Europe; even as far away as Iceland. Three of the sections of his book on falconry concern gerfalcons, which he secured through Lubeck from Norway and Iceland. Other falcons came from Malta. It is clear that Frederick enjoyed the opportunity to regularly obtain falcons from within his empire and beyond.

Frederick initiated his sons Manfred and Enzio into falconry. Manfred became a well-known falconer, and Enzio was known to hunt with falcons. Manfred, at some point in the 1240s, asked his father to put all his knowledge into written form. The resulting book, *De arte venandi cum avibus*, is still in print. It is an example of Frederick's being well ahead of his times in the ability to conduct scientific observation. The book was completed by 1248, when one full copy was captured by Frederick's enemies while looting his camp outside Parma. There were no printing presses, so few copies of any new book existed, but Frederick had other manuscripts prepared. After Frederick's death, Manfred updated one of the manuscripts with notes of his own. This is the manuscript that came down to the Vatican Library, where it is one of the treasures of a great collection.

The Art of Falconry is written in six books. The extant manuscripts are either of all six books or a version with just the first two books. Frederick makes reference to other works he had written on diseases of falcons, and also on hunting with hawks. These works are lost. What remains shows an unusual attitude toward nature for the thirteenth century. The normal works on animals during this time were called bestiaries, and they were mostly a gathering of legends and myths about various animals. Frederick was determined to only record what he had seen with his own eyes, or verified by talk with other falconers he trusted. He refers to Aristotle mostly to point out where his own observations differed from the philosopher's. Frederick, unlike most scholars in the Middle Ages, took to heart Aristotle's admonition to verify and observe before asserting. If he spotted discrepancies between what he saw and what Aristotle wrote, he believed his eyes, not Aristotle's words. This was unusual for the time, given the canon-like authority of the great philosopher's works.

The first section of *The Art of Falconry* is titled "The Structure and Habits of Birds." The quality of observation is outstanding, and it is easy to see why this work has survived. Frederick used his own classification system, which was land, water, and neutral (both land and water) birds, and came up with differences and similarities between them. With our current superior methods of observation, some of Frederick's "facts" have been proven wrong. But considering that he made his observations using thirteenth century technology, the level of accuracy is very high. This first section of the book deals with general knowledge about birds, not with birds of prey specifically.

The second section deals specifically with falcons. Frederick had over thirty years of experience with these birds by this time, and it shows. He discusses the various types of falcons used for hunting—their habits and hunting methods in the wild—and how to capture a falcon. The next portion of this section is about training a falcon to get it ready to learn to hunt for a human. It is very detailed and covers not just the bird but all the accoutrements needed (including furniture, cages, hoods, and jesses) to train a falcon. A large portion of this section has to do with seeling, or sewing the eyelids together to blind the bird. This was done to allow the falcon to become accustomed to humans, which was easier if the bird could not see the falconer. Frederick had learned on his trip to the Holy Land a new

Illustrations from an edition of *The Art of Falconry*. The top accompanies Frederick's discussion of bird feet while the bottom illustrates his observations about bird necks. (*Art of Falconry [1943]*)

method of blinding an untrained falcon, the use of a hood. Frederick introduced this to Europe, and in the final part of this section he deals with the use of the hood. It is an interesting example of someone who is thoroughly trained in an old and valid way of doing something coming to terms with a new, better way. He is not totally convinced, but he sees the efficacy of the new method.

The third section discusses how to prepare the falcon for the hunt. Here Frederick deals with lures, and the use of dogs along with the falcons. The procedures outlined in this section are designed to get the falcons used to the presence of humans, horses, and dogs while on a hunt, obviously something not experienced by a falcon in the wild. Again, the observations are very detailed, the products of long experience.

The rest of the book has to do with specific falcons hunting specific prey. Two sections are about hunting cranes and herons with larger falcons. Those kinds of hunting are no longer practiced today, so the accuracy of Frederick's observations cannot be judged. The final section, though, has to do with the hunting of smaller waterfowl such as ducks and geese with peregrine falcons. That activity is still practiced, and Frederick's observations are still valid.

The Art of Falconry grew out of Frederick's special status as a ruler. He goes over, in his introduction, the four types of people who hunt with falcons, and writes: "Here it may again be claimed that, since many nobles and but few of the lower rank learn and carefully pursue this art, one may properly conclude that it is intrinsically an aristocratic sport, and one may once more add that it is nobler, more worthy than, and superior to other kinds of hunting."[3] This is just another indication of the fact that Frederick was very conscious of rank. Another story, again possibly apocryphal, illustrates this point with birds. Frederick was training a falcon that was sent off to make a kill. The falcon crossed the path of a newly fledged eagle and killed it. When the eagle was brought to Frederick, he had the falcon killed. In Frederick's eyes, eagles outranked falcons, and a falcon had no business killing an eagle.[4]

3. Frederick II of Hohenstaufen, *The Art of Falconry*, trans. Casey A. Wood (Stanford, 1943), 6.

4. Patience Andrewes, *Frederick II of Hohenstaufen* (London, 1970), 34.

Illustrations showing the correct way of handling a falcon, top, and securing a falcon to a post. (*Art of Falconry* [1943])

It is unfortunate that Frederick's other works, on bird diseases and hawking, were lost. *The Art of Falconry* shows his great ability as an ornithologist and his skill in being able to organize a work into a readable book. It is an indication of how much slower-paced life was in the thirteenth century that someone as prominent as Frederick could find the time to make and organize the observations in *The Art of Falconry*. As he states in the introduction, "As the ruler of a large kingdom and an extensive empire we were very often hampered by arduous and intricate governmental duties, but despite these handicaps we did not lay aside our self-imposed task and were successful in committing to writing at the proper time the elements of this art."[5]

Having acknowledged Frederick's accomplishments as an observer of birds, we now return to his activities as a ruler.

5. Frederick II, *The Art of Falconry*, 3.

EIGHT

Tightening the Reins

FREDERICK HAD ARRANGED TO HAVE his eldest son, Henry, elected king of the Germans before he left Germany in 1220. At that time, Henry was still a minor, so Frederick designated the archbishop of Cologne as regent. The archbishop was also to be Henry's guardian. The parallels with Frederick's own life are remarkable. Frederick had no relationship with his father and a prematurely cut off relationship with his mother. It appears Henry had the same experience. He only knew his father for four years in Germany, at a time when Frederick was busy establishing his status as emperor. Henry never saw his mother after 1220, communicating only by letter. Henry also shared with his father the experience of being raised by churchmen, and probably resenting it.

Frederick had shown during his residence in Germany that he was willing to rule the empire with loose reins. Frederick confirmed the rights of secular and spiritual lords, only asking that they acknowledge him as overlord and come to his aid when asked. This loose grip had served Frederick well, even during the worst of his disputes with the pope. Gregory IX tried to recruit lords in Germany to lead an opposition to Frederick, but the effort failed, as the lords of the empire remained loyal. This allowed Frederick to concentrate on the crusade and the kingdom for the decade of the 1220s.

REBELLION OF HENRY

The regency of the archbishop of Cologne came to an end in 1225, when he was assassinated by one of his own relations. During his regency, the archbishop had turned Henry over to be trained by some of the *ministeriales* in Henry's ancestral home of Swabia. These *ministeriales* were Henry's daily companions. They appear to have implanted in him the idea that a Hohenstaufen did not have to allow the great lords of the empire the rights that had been granted by his father. These *ministeriales* were often at odds with the spiritual lords of the empire as well. Frederick was aware of this, and on the death of the archbishop, he named a secular lord, Ludwig, Duke of Bavaria, as the new regent. To further tighten ties to the secular lords, Frederick arranged the marriage of Henry to the daughter of the duke of Austria.

That was how matters stood until Frederick went off on crusade. Then, in 1228, Henry threw off the rule of the regent, and as a result his father-in-law also left court. Henry was well past the age when Frederick had assumed authority; there was no denying he had the right to assume personal rule. Henry had absorbed enough of the beliefs of his *ministeriales* to initiate actions that caused him trouble. In 1229, Henry gathered an army and marched into the territory of the duke of Bavaria. He was not trying to destroy the duke but to get a firm pledge of loyalty. Ludwig complied under duress, which he did not feel was binding. By his actions in 1229 and early 1230, Henry made it clear to the secular and spiritual lords that the main decision-making power would be concentrated in him, without much consultation with the lords. He issued imperial privileges to some towns that did not enjoy them before, such as Nijmegen, in what is now the Netherlands. This was against the policy of the emperor, who had not done this while in Germany.

Henry and the leading lords of the empire met twice, at diets of Worms in 1230 and 1231. The lords contacted Frederick and won him over to their side. Frederick then promulgated the *Contitutio in favorem principum* (Constitution to Aid our Rule), which made clear the relationship of the lords and the king of the Germans. Frederick came down on the side of the lords, against his son. He then called all parties to meet with him at the Diet of Ravenna in northeast Italy in November 1231. Frederick meant to settle the dispute and also show the flag in the Lombard area. The Lombard towns that were against Frederick again blockaded the passes of the Alps to keep as many of the German lords as they could from attending the diet. Many lords made it through; Henry did not.

Frederick was not pleased, and called for a new diet at Aquileia, about fifty miles east of Venice on the Adriatic coast, in May 1232. Frederick did not return to the Kingdom of Sicily during this time, but went around to the loyal Lombard towns and made a state visit to Venice, which enjoyed good relations with Frederick at this time. He showed off his menagerie to the northern Italians, and indulged in his love of hunting. He sent messages to Henry that he was displeased and expected him to attend the next diet.

Henry arrived in Aquileia in May 1232. He was assigned quarters several miles outside town, an indication of how his father viewed him. With the intercession of several German princes, Frederick and Henry reached an agreement, the main point of which was that Henry should not overstep the bounds of accepted practice of ruling the empire. Henry was again made aware that he was subordinate to the emperor, and that Frederick did not want him upsetting the peace of the German portion of the empire. Frederick had enough problems in Sicily and Lombardy, and he did not want to spend much time dealing with Germany. In a ceremony at the conclusion of the diet, Henry vowed to obey his father.

However, Henry resented his treatment by his father, whom he hardly knew. From 1232 through 1234, Henry followed the agreement. But because of a dispute with the new Bavarian duke, Henry invaded Bavaria. The duke had been attempting to annex some of Henry's Swabian lands. Henry's actions were justified, and this was confirmed by the surrendering of the duke's eight-year-old heir as a hostage as part of the peace agreement. Henry became more dissatisfied with his status as time went on. He took a step in 1235 that showed the seriousness of his rebellion: he signed a pact, against his father, with the Lombard League.

RETURN TO GERMANY

In the past, the Lombard League's main ally in its struggles against Frederick had been the pope. But Frederick's relationship with Gregory IX was cordial at this time, mostly because Frederick helped Gregory with his problems with the Roman populace. So when the Lombards turned to Henry, Frederick decided the only way to clear up the situation was to return to Germany.

Frederick had not been north of the Alps since 1220. When he went the first time, he was counting on the power of his name to tip the balance. Now he was accompanied by a small army and was counting on the loyalty of the princes. Frederick reached Regensburg in May 1235, and held a court of all the powerful princes and bishops. Henry did not attend, as he was busy besieging the city of Worms, which was loyal to Frederick. After news of Frederick's appearance in Germany reached Henry's army, it melted away. Henry was persuaded to submit to the emperor. He was placed under arrest, to await the arrival of Frederick in Worms. The political and diplomatic isolation effected by the emperor was too much for Henry to overcome.

This isolation had started the year before. Frederick had taken his second legitimate son, Conrad, to meet the pope. Frederick offered to leave Conrad as a hostage, but he also said he intended for Conrad to be the new king of the Germans. Pope Gregory and Frederick agreed on the excommunication of many of Frederick's enemies, which included several Lombard communes—and Henry. Gregory promulgated the excommunication of Henry in July 1234, along with instructions that Henry no longer be recognized as king. This deposition set a dangerous precedent for Frederick in the future, but he was pleased with it now.

Henry had been trying to secure the support of the French, long-time allies of Frederick's. Word of Henry's efforts reached the pope and Frederick, and they came up with a plan to counteract this. Gregory thought a new marriage alliance with England would help. The English king, Henry III, had a sister who was in her twentieth year. Frederick decided to consider this. He sent Piero della Vigna on a mission to London to determine if the girl was suitable and to negotiate the marriage settlement. The agreement was executed in early 1235, and Isabella of England set off for Cologne in May 1235.

Frederick reached Worms in July 1235. He held court on July 4. Henry was brought to court, and threw himself at the emperor's feet. Frederick continued to do business with the nobles over Henry's prostrate body, until the nobles asked Frederick to notice Henry's presence. The political theater played out with Frederick issuing terms of settlement. The terms included recognition of the deposition of Henry from his throne, and the turning over of all symbols of authority. Henry refused these terms and was imprisoned. He was first sent to prison in the Duchy of Bavaria, and eventually moved to the Kingdom of Sicily. Henry played no more role in either the empire or the kingdom. He was still in prison in the kingdom when, in 1242, Frederick called for Henry to be brought to him. On the way, Henry saw a chance for permanent escape: near Mortorano, he threw himself off a mountain road to his death. Frederick claimed afterward that he had been calling Henry back to forgive him and show some mercy. He issued a circular letter to the Sicilian nobility, citing the story of Absalom from the Bible as an example of how he felt about this turn of events.

It was clear that Frederick and Henry never agreed on how to rule Germany. Frederick made his arrangements during the decade of the 1210s to keep the peace and let the German princes handle the day-to-day ruling of this part of the empire. Henry—in the manner of sons of kings from Absalom to Henry II and George III of England—wanted more authority than he was given. Aside from the fact that he really did not know his father, he was influenced by his surroundings in Germany. During this time, Frederick wanted to concentrate on the kingdom and Lombardy, and keep Germany quiet. Some German historians take Henry's side in this dispute, for he was trying to concentrate more power in the hands of the king than the princes. Frederick did not think that process would work in Germany, so he denounced and deposed his son.

After the deposition of Henry, Frederick needed to beget more legitimate sons. He already had several illegitimate sons, but they could not hope to inherit his realms. His son Conrad had accompanied Frederick to Germany and was being introduced to all the nobility as their next king. With his marriage to Isabella of England on July 20, 1235, came the hope for more sons. Frederick was pleased with Isabella but had consulted astrologers before the wedding. On their advice, he waited until the second night to consummate the marriage. He then dismissed her suite of ladies, saying that his court would take care of Isabella until she delivered the son he desired. Isabella gave birth to a daughter nearly nine months later. She gave birth to a son, also named Henry, in 1238. She then gave birth to a stillborn son in 1239, and she died soon afterward. During her time with Frederick, she was confined, as her predecessor Isabella of Jerusalem had been, to the women's quarters. She was never crowned empress and took no part in ruling.

After the wedding, Frederick had held a diet at Mainz. He met with the nobles who had come for the prior meeting and the wedding. He confirmed their rights and received renewed vows of loyalty. Again, Frederick made no effort to assert his power over Germany. He wanted the support of the nobles, not their submission, as he demanded in the kingdom.

Another incident was resolved at this time. Earlier, several Jews in Hagenau had been accused of a ritual murder of a Christian child, a common charge of this time. Frederick had appointed a special court to consider the matter, and the court had concluded that it needed to know more about the Jewish religion before making its decision. Frederick wanted to consult with any converted Jew in his domain who could explain Jewish religious practices to him. He discovered that no one in Germany would admit to this, so he had to send to England for converted Jews. King Henry III sent him two men. These converts proved conclusively to Frederick that Jewish law had absolute abhorrence of any human sacrifice. Hence, he acquitted the charged parties and issued an edict forbidding any more charges of this sort. This worked in Frederick's lifetime, but European history is littered with subsequent examples of this charge.

After this action, and on his way back to Italy, Frederick stopped in Marburg to participate in some religious ceremonies. When Frederick left on crusade the first time, the disease that struck his army killed his friend the margrave of Thuringia. This death turned the margrave's wife, Elizabeth, into a woman of extreme holiness. Her fasting and denial of the flesh led to her death a short time after the death of the margrave. She was viewed as a saint by the locals. After the normal process of canonization, the church declared her a saint. Frederick attended the ceremonies in Marburg installing Elizabeth as a saint. Her marriage to the margrave had made Elizabeth a second cousin of Frederick's. His participation was to honor a friend, relative, and subject all at once. This ceremony also reflected glory on the ruler who had harbored this saint. Frederick's participation, whatever his own religious views, made good political sense.

In 1237, Frederick made one more short trip north of the Alps. He led an imperial procession through Austria, where Duke Frederick had been in rebellion. The emperor isolated the duke in the castle of Wiener Neustadt in the winter of 1237–38. Frederick spent that winter in Vienna, and awarded imperial privileges to the city. He was also able to gather enough of the princes of the empire to settle the succession of the empire now that Henry had been deposed. The princes elected Conrad, Frederick's only other legitimate son at this time, as king of the

Romans. In addition to resolving the succession of the empire, the electors wished to show the pope that the making and breaking of emperors was not in the Vatican's power, but in the hands of the electors.

After 1238, Frederick never returned to his domains north of the Alps. He appointed first the archbishop of Mainz, then Henry Raspe of Thuringia, as regent for Conrad. These arrangements remained until Conrad came of age, which happened by 1242. Conrad always kept in contact with Frederick and did not follow in the rebellious footsteps of his half-brother Henry. Frederick wanted just a few things from the non-Italian part of the empire. One was peace, and he was willing to concede rights and privileges to the lay and spiritual lords to get it. This strategy, while not serving the purpose of centralization of power, worked over the course of Frederick's life. The other thing he wanted was fighting men from the northern domains to aid him in his conflicts with the Lombards. Frederick was always able to get some men from Germany for his forces. These troops were being used, along with local forces from Italy, in Lombardy.

CONFLICT IN LOMBARDY

Frederick had returned from crusade and reestablished his authority in the kingdom by the end of 1230. He had not had any major dealings with the Lombard communes since before he had gone to the Holy Land. When he went north to hold diets at Ravenna and Aquileia, the Lombard communes were asked to send representatives. The Ghibelline communes, such as Cremona and Verona, sent representatives; the members of the Lombard League, led by Milan, did not. These Guelf communes also took the step of blocking the Alpine passes to keep German representatives from attending the diets. This strategy worked for the Diet of Ravenna in 1231, but not for the Diet of Aquileia in 1232. At Aquileia, with the pope's approval, Frederick declared a ban of empire on the communes that did not attend. This act revoked privileges, but was only enforceable by an army. As we have seen, Frederick was concentrating on the affairs of the kingdom from 1229 through 1234, and he spent most of 1235 in Germany. No action was taken against the banned communes before early 1236.

Frederick had been consulting with Pope Gregory IX about his policy in Lombardy, as the emperor and pope were allied at this time. Frederick wrote the pope from Germany in August 1235 that the German princes were going to contribute troops to assist the emperor on an expedition to Lombardy. The pope urged the emperor and the communes to negotiate, which Frederick was happy to do. Gregory organized a conference, to be mediated by himself, in Rome in December 1235. Frederick sent his trusted envoy, Hermann von Salza, to be his representative. He let the Lombards know what his terms would be. After learning the terms, the Lombard League met in November 1235. Its members reaffirmed their resistance to the emperor. They also recruited another member, the town of Ferrara. This was a concern for Frederick, as Ferrara lay on the road from Verona to the south. Ferrara could block land access to the kingdom from northeast Italy. Neither Frederick nor the Lombards attended the conference in Rome, and the conference failed. The result was the start of an active conflict.

Gregory and Frederick had kept the agreement they reached in 1230 for six years. Frederick had kept the pope informed of all his actions in Italy and Germany during this time. Frederick had also secured the pope's approval for dealing with his son Henry. The pope had issued an interdict on the Lombard cities during this time. Now the pope decided that his peace efforts were not going to work, and he was going to have to choose a side in the conflict between Frederick and the Lombards. The indicator as to which side he would take came in summer 1236. The pope relieved his serving representative to the Lombard communes and appointed James of Palestrina. James was a known opponent of Frederick's in the Curia. Frederick had called for a diet at Piacenza for late 1236. James, a native of Piacenza, went there immediately. He convinced Piacenza to change its allegiance from Frederick to the Lombard League. Frederick saw this as a threat to his plans in Lombardy, and wrote to his fellow rulers in England and France of the injustice of the attitude of the pope.

Frederick's dispute with the Lombard communes was that they would not honor his authority as emperor. If there was one thing Frederick was not, it was a democrat. Frederick believed that he and other rulers were God's secular representatives on Earth and that any rebellion against him was a rebellion against God.

The communities in Lombardy (and in Tuscany just south) had, since the eleventh century, developed a form of self-government. Readers of Renaissance history are familiar with the despotism exercised in the fifteenth and sixteenth centuries by leaders like the Sforza, Medici, Este, and other families. Each of these towns started with an oligarchic government not recognizable as a democracy by modern standards. More than one person or family participated in the rule of the towns, which usually had at least two factions, labeled at the time as Guelf (antiemperor) and Ghibelline (proemperor). The towns could, and did, change allegiances. This was decided by which faction was in control, and how strong the various armed forces were in their neighborhood. Throughout the Lombard conflict with Frederick, the local disputes within and between towns were more important to the people in those towns than were the larger disputes between the emperor and the Lombard League or the pope.

One community in Lombardy had already made the step from participatory government to despotism. That was Verona, and the duke there, Ezzelino da Romano, became a strong ally of Frederick's. Ezzelino was a formidable fighter, a good general, and one of the most vilified characters of his time. He was such a consistent enemy of the papacy that a crusade was launched against him in 1254. Ezzelino fought for Frederick until the emperor died, committed brutal acts against his enemies, and poured public scorn on the church.

Verona was the first stop Frederick made in summer 1236 in Lombardy. Ezzelino got Frederick involved in a feud with his main enemy, Azzo d'Este. Ezzelino and Azzo (who was allied to the Lombard League at this time) were competing for control of the towns in the mainland opposite Venice. The imperial army and Ezzelino's forces were camped on one side of the Adige River, with Azzo's forces camped on the other. The imperial army appeared to leave, heading west to Cremona. Azzo's force was now confident and prepared to attack Ezzelino. But Azzo's force was slow, and Frederick's forces returned and confronted Azzo with both armies. Azzo's forces ran away without a fight, opening the way to Vicenza, one of the towns in dispute between Ezzelino and Azzo. Vicenza was besieged and taken in August 1236. Frederick and Ezzelino did not sack the town but set fire to it to impress other towns in the area that they could save themselves by changing sides.

Frederick at this point hoped that the taking of Vicenza would be compelling enough to bring the Lombards around. He pursued diplomatic avenues and got a turnaround in the allegiance of Ferrara, which went over to Frederick's side in

October 1236. This was welcome, but in the current climate of Italian rivalries, it eventually cost Frederick the friendship of Venice. In November 1236, Frederick was confident enough of the state of affairs in Lombardy to leave Italy for Austria, as discussed above. His diplomacy to the pope had resulted in the recall of Cardinal James of Palestrina and his replacement with more moderate papal representatives to the Lombards. These legates arranged a conference at Brescia in July 1237. Frederick sent Hermann von Salza and Piero della Vigna to this conference. Frederick insisted on terms that the Lombards, with papal concurrence, would not agree to. Hence, Frederick returned to Lombardy in mid-September 1237, ready for renewed conflict. The pope was in the background calling for the renewal of a crusade because the truce between Frederick and al-Kamil was going to expire soon. The pope wanted to permanently secure Jerusalem. He was also building his case against Frederick, and biding his time.

Both the Lombards and Frederick ignored the papal chorus. The army of the emperor was now augmented by troops recruited in Germany, from the Ghibelline towns, and by Muslim units that had been called north from the kingdom. Frederick led this army from Mantua toward Cremona, accepting the submission of several towns on the route. The Lombards had constructed a fortified camp at Pontevico, to protect the town of Brescia. Frederick attempted to draw the Lombard troops, who were mostly from Milan, out of the camp into battle, but was unsuccessful. In November 1237, Frederick started a troop movement that seemed to indicate his army was going into winter camp in Cremona, just south of Pontevico. The Milanese thought this would be the end of the campaign and started a troop movement of their own toward Milan. But Frederick had left a detachment behind to alert him the moment the enemy broke camp. Frederick turned his army around after hearing the news and led a forced march that caught the Milanese in the open near Cortenuova. The resulting battle, one of the few Frederick was able to force with the Lombards, was a convincing victory for the emperor. The imperial troops inflicted more than two thousand casualties on a force of about twelve thousand, and captured many other troops. The captured included the podesta of Milan, the highest judicial officer; and the son of the current doge of Venice. Also captured was the carroccio of Milan, an ox-drawn cart that contained the sacred relics and banners of the city and was taken by Milanese troops into battle as a morale booster.

After this victory, Frederick went into winter quarters in the friendly town of Cremona. On his entry there, a triumph in the ancient Roman style was celebrated. This was further evidence of Frederick's vision of the Holy Roman Empire as the successor to the original Roman Empire. During this winter, the Lombard League lost strength. Some towns, such as Lodi, changed allegiance to the emperor. Frederick had notified Gregory of his victories, which did not please the pope. However, Gregory was in no position to defy the emperor, and went along with his plans. Frederick opened negotiations with the Lombards in December 1237. The Lombards' terms were recognition of Frederick's sovereignty without loss of communal and territorial rights, provision of ten thousand men to go on crusade, and a monetary fine, with the amount to be agreed on. Frederick countered with a demand for the unconditional surrender of Milan. He did not promise to destroy the city or even sack it, but he insisted Milan must be at his mercy. Not surprisingly, the Milanese did not agree.

Milan's collective memory reached back seventy years. In a similar situation, Frederick's grandfather Barbarossa had razed

The Battle of Cortenuova. Frederick was able to catch and defeat an army from Milan at Cortenuova. Some Milanese troops who were able to escape, and made their way back to the fortified city of Milan.

Milan. The Milanese thought Frederick's attitude toward the communes was similar to his grandfather's. Frederick did not expect to sweep away all the rights and privileges of the communes; evidence of that had been shown by his governance in Germany. The towns that were loyal to the empire, such as Cremona, had been confirmed in their rights. At this time, it appears Frederick's plan was to impose tighter control than had existed. But he was not planning to dissolve the communes and take away all their rights. The Milanese did not dispute that the emperor was their overlord, but wanted no other relationship with the empire. They had seen that the emperor was appointing podestas, usually Sicilian barons, to administer conquered Lombard cities. Milan was slowly following the path of Venice, which claimed to be independent of the empire.

In the spring of 1238, Frederick resumed his campaign. He determined that a siege of Milan would be too difficult and decided to conquer the second-largest Guelf commune in the area, Brescia. Frederick had gathered and financed a larger army than his army of the year before, with contributions coming from as far as England. Ezzelino had procured the services of a Spanish expert, Calamandrino, to construct and operate the siege machines. The siege started in July 1238. Unfortunately for imperial forces, at some point the Brescians captured Calamandrino. Offers of money and a wife led him into their service, and his advice had a major effect on the siege. Though the siege became brutal on both sides, the Brescians were not discouraged in their resistance. In November 1238, Frederick returned to winter quarters in Cremona. He did not acknowledge the fact, but it was clear that the siege had failed. The members of the Ghibelline faction of Brescia left town, went to the emperor, and were awarded lands in Sicily. Other towns in the area switched back to Guelf loyalty. Genoa, which had been harboring a grievance against Frederick since 1220, formally broke with him.

The most important power Frederick had to deal with was the pope. Gregory IX was still maintaining his neutrality and peaceful intentions in this dispute, but those intentions were changing. In summer 1238, Gregory appointed another clerical enemy of Frederick's, Gregorio di Montelongo, as papal representative to the Lombards. He became, and stayed, a source of irritation to the emperor. The emperor struck back in Sardinia. The pope considered the island to be a papal territory, but possession really was disputed between Genoa and Pisa. Parts of northern Sardinia had a princess, Adalasia, who was a widow. The pope had proposed a marriage for her to a close ally of his. At the same time, the emperor proposed a marriage to his illegitimate son Enzio. It appears Adalasia actually met both men and made up her own mind. Even though she was threatened with excommunication by the pope, she chose Enzio. Enzio and Adalasia were crowned king and queen of Sardinia (an expansion of her actual domain, which was just the northern part of the island). The couple then went to Frederick's court, where they spent the rest of their lives, never returning to Sardinia. Enzio became vicar-general for Lombardy for his father and a leading military leader in the imperial forces.

Later in the winter of 1238–39, Frederick and his forces made an imperial progress through loyal areas to Padua, where they spent the rest of the winter. Frederick tried to reconcile the families of Ezzelino and the d'Este by marrying Ezzelino's son to a niece of Azzo d'Este's. This worked, but only for the short term. The d'Este family had wavered between the pope and the emperor, and would continue to do so. Frederick also became aware that Pope Gregory was gathering ammunition against him and preparing another excommunication. While Frederick knew he could survive another excommunication, he did not want to have to deal with it. There was much correspondence between the Curia and Frederick's court, mostly handled by Piero della Vigna on Frederick's behalf. Charges were exchanged, and the pope's decision was awaited.

NINE

Challenges Closer to Home

POPE GREGORY IX IMPOSED his second sentence of excommunication on Frederick on Palm Sunday 1239. The pope's explanation of his action did not address Lombard affairs. There were many other charges having to do with Frederick holding lands in the Papal States and preventing papal representatives from traveling to their assigned areas. Frederick was also charged with neglecting the defense of Jerusalem. And he was charged with keeping a Tunisian prince in captivity and preventing him from being baptized. This was part of a larger charge of interfering with the activities of the church in the kingdom. This dispute went back to the renunciation of rights by Frederick's mother during Frederick's minority. Frederick had never really recognized this renunciation, and it was a continual source of conflict. Ironically, on the date of this excommunication, Frederick's most trusted and effective envoy to the papacy, Hermann von Salza, died. Hermann never learned of the final break between the two powers he tried to reconcile.

The pope did not confine his attacks on the emperor to his own words. He sent out friars to spread the word and to release the emperor's subjects from their allegiance. During this era, news spread slowly, and there were no public means of communication. The church enjoyed a near monopoly on literacy and used that position to vilify the emperor. The pope sent direct communications to the other rulers of Europe justifying his actions. He sent papal representatives more committed to the policy against Frederick to the Lombard cities in an attempt to change the allegiance of the towns that had submitted to Frederick. The emissary to Milan, Gregorio di Montelongo, went so far as to declare a crusade against Frederick. The pope did not ratify the declaration, but anything short of that was allowed. The pope also imposed increased tithes on churches in France, Spain, Germany, and England to fund these activities.

Frederick did not take this lying down. He had been gathering literate, secular servants to his court, taking advantage of the operation of the University of Naples. Frederick's current right-hand man, Piero della Vigna, was the leader of a new propaganda effort. With Frederick looking on from his throne, Piero delivered an oration in Padua justifying Frederick's behavior and attacking the pope. Letters were sent to the other rulers of Europe, again stating that Frederick had behaved correctly, and that the pope was not correct in his actions. He called Gregory an impure priest, unjust judge, and unseeing prophet. He also warned the other crowned heads of Europe that this attack on the imperial crown would be followed by attacks on their own crowns.

Henry III of England sided with the pope but was not able to collect much of the money that had been requested because of the opposition of his barons. Louis IX of France (later to be St. Louis) did not agree with the pope, claiming he had exceeded his authority. Louis said a church council was necessary to condemn a crowned head. Germany, where the pope sent many friars to arouse opposition to Frederick, remained loyal to the emperor.

These were the public results of the propaganda war. The private condemnations on both sides reached a level of polemic not often seen. Papal correspondence with other churchmen called Frederick "forerunner of the Antichrist."[1] The old charge that he was not a practicing Christian was dusted off and stressed. His immorality was reviewed, citing all his illegitimate children. With no evidence, he was called a sodomite. A charge that had been leveled against supposed unbelievers since the eleventh century was used against Frederick: that he denied the Virgin Birth and had called Moses, Jesus, and Muhammad the three imposters. Added to this was the charge of being too friendly to Islam and Judaism. Consistency was not important to the Curia in the propaganda war.

The vast majority of clergy in Frederick's realms walked the tightrope of staying loyal to Frederick and the church. There were few defections among the higher clergy of the kingdom or empire from Frederick to the pope. Archbishop Berard had been loyal to Frederick from the start, and remained so throughout the continuing conflict with the pope. Frederick gained a notable religious ally in Elias of Cortona. Elias was the minister-general of the Franciscan order. Elias had known St. Francis and had been an early follower of his. Francis and Elias had different personalities, and took different paths. St. Francis realized early on that he had no administrative abilities and

---

1. Van Cleve, *The Emperor Frederick II*, 431.

turned over the running of the order to Elias. Elias respected St. Francis's ideas, particularly in his condemnation of the autocracy of the church and Curia. However, Elias did not practice poverty and piety like Francis. Elias wanted the order to become influential in the world and the church. He was aware that Frederick respected St. Francis. An alliance between the Franciscan order and Frederick was reached. Elias was eventually excommunicated by the pope as well. Elias then absolved all those whom the pope had excommunicated.

During the campaigning season of 1239, Frederick remained in Lombardy. He brought a large army to the vicinity of Milan and tried to lure the Milanese out of their fortress. This did not succeed; the Milanese were not having a battle in the open after Cortenuova. Frederick remained in this area until October, when he gave up this hope and started moving south.

During the summer of 1239, various Lombard towns changed allegiance. Frederick was able to gain Como and Monza, but lost Bologna and Treviso. The chessboard of Guelf-Ghibelline allegiance in Lombardy was constantly changing. More important was the three-way alliance of the pope, Genoa, and Venice. Agreement was reached among the three in 1239. The pope wanted the maritime powers to supply shipping for an invasion of the kingdom. The maritime powers agreed and were now waiting for the pope to come up with troops for the invasion. Frederick was moving down the western part of the peninsula to deal with this threat. He had already sent forces led by Enzio down the eastern part of the peninsula. Enzio was dealing with papal forces in the March of Ancona, and pushing those forces south. Frederick made progress through Tuscany, then entered papal territory in the Duchy of Spoleto. All that territory submitted to Frederick, except the towns of Perugia, Assisi, Spoleto, and Terni.

By February 1240, Frederick had reached Viterbo in the Patrimony of St. Peter. Pope Gregory IX was in Rome, whose citizens were still displeased with him and tended to support the emperor. Frederick brought his army to the vicinity of Rome and awaited the opening of the city gates to allow him entry. Gregory knew he was in a difficult situation. Even in his late eighties, the pope remained defiant of the emperor. Gregory turned the situation around with an effective bit of religious and political theater. On February 22, Gregory led all ranks of clergy—from local church leaders to members of the papal bureaucracy—in a procession from the Lateran Palace to St. Peter's. The Ghibelline supporters of Frederick's hooted at the procession and surrounded the pope on the steps of St. Peter's. Gregory spoke to the crowd, exhibiting holy relics (purportedly the skulls of St. Peter and St. Paul), and taking his papal tiara and putting it on one of the skulls. He proclaimed a holy war against the emperor, urging the Romans to protect the liberty of the church. The fickle Roman crowd changed its mind and backed the pope. The gates of Rome remained closed.

Frederick knew that for political and military reasons he could not take Rome by siege, so he moved south and returned to the kingdom. Frederick had supporters in the College of Cardinals and hoped to eventually negotiate a workable settlement with the pope.

In 1240, both sides took their next steps in the dispute. Frederick returned to the Papal States, but only in transit with his army. Frederick was heading to the Romagna region to attempt to win back the allegiance of some of the towns in that province, which was nominally supposed to be ruled by the pope. It was a sign of papal weakness that Frederick met no resistance until he got to the towns involved. He had sent a new emissary to the pope, the new head of the Teutonic Knights,

Conrad of Thuringia. Frederick's friends in the College of Cardinals were also being heard in Rome.

Pope Gregory's response was to call a general council of the church at Rome for Easter 1241, to take action against the emperor. Frederick did not dispute that course, but Frederick's clerical supporters and the pope disagreed on the composition of the council. The pope wanted Lombard representation, and the emperor wanted to limit any such participation. Members of the College of Cardinals, led by Cardinal Giovanni Colonna, urged the pope to negotiate and consider the emperor's position. Gregory refused, and according to contemporary English chronicler Matthew Paris, he had a violent quarrel with Colonna. The cardinal then became more Ghibelline in his sympathies and led the opposition to the pope within the Curia.

Frederick allowed the higher clergy from his realms to attend the council, but he did not guarantee the safe passage of other clergy there. Frederick was in Romagna keeping his lines of communication to northeast Italy open in the winter of 1240–41. Frederick appointed a Genoese loyal to him, Ansaldus di Mari, as admiral of Sicily and instructed him to intercept as many of the delegates to the council as he could. The delegates from northern Europe and Lombardy had gathered in Genoa, and a Genoese fleet escorted the delegates to Rome. Ansaldus learned of this, and with a fleet of Sicilian and Pisan galleys, he intercepted the Genoese fleet off the coast of Tuscany. The result was a decisive victory for Frederick: the Genoese fleet was destroyed, and two cardinals and many archbishops and bishops were captured.

Frederick ordered the imprisonment of the captured clergy, hoping to use them as bargaining chips with Gregory. He was gratified by the capture of a long-time enemy, Cardinal James of Palestrina. The confinement of James became another papal charge against Frederick in the summer of 1241. Frederick had finished his military actions in northeast Italy and was returning to the kingdom through the Patrimony of St. Peter. Frederick was in contact with Cardinal Colonna, still trying to negotiate a settlement with Gregory. Gregory was not responding in any way, and the presence of imperial armies in the neighborhood of Rome kept him confined to the city. Pope Gregory IX, who was in his early nineties, fell ill in the summer heat and died in August 1241.

At some point in his career as a cardinal, Gregory had turned against the emperor. He became the leader of the papal opposition to Frederick while still a cardinal. After a tactical retreat from 1230 to 1239, Gregory continued his verbal and military opposition to the emperor that had started with Frederick's first excommunication. The assertion of papal authority over temporal rulers was the main dispute between Frederick and Gregory. Gregory continued the policy of his mentor, Pope Innocent III, that the Donation of Constantine gave the pope authority over all temporal rulers. Gregory also tried to keep Frederick's realms separate, as Innocent III had tried. At the time of his death, Gregory had not defeated Frederick.

Frederick was in a good political position, but the status of this conflict would depend on the selection of the next pope, which will be discussed in the next chapter.

RULING THE KINGDOM

For much of his reign, Frederick's methods of ruling can only be inferred from laws, edicts, and actions. But for the period October 1239 through May 1240, there is documentary proof of how he ruled the kingdom: a 116-page register of letters written from the court (which was in various places) to officials in the kingdom. This register was used by all my sources, and explored in detail by David Abulafia. This register had been held in the archives of Naples and had been saved by the actions of several archivists and scholars. The original was destroyed along with everything else in the archive by German troops in 1943, but copies of the register had been transferred to microfilm, and they were uncovered after the war.

It is not known who actually wrote the letters, which are in Latin. This is not the ornate Latin used by both sides in the propaganda war between the emperor and the pope, but business Latin, probably taken from Frederick in dictation and then transcribed by the actual writer of the document. Many subjects are covered, although letters dealing with the conflict with the papacy are rare. Letters dealing with the nitty-gritty of government are much more common. These show that Frederick had borrowed money from Roman bankers for his recent actions in the vicinity of Rome. Frederick was always concerned with paying back loans because he knew he would have to borrow again. Hence, many letters are about raising money in the kingdom. He got regular financial reports from his realm, which was his main source of funds for his conflicts with the Lombards and the papacy. He made inquiries into assets and liabilities in the kingdom, such as the wheat stocks and sheep flocks. Frederick did not mortgage his resources to the bankers, but because he was short of ready cash, he took many short-term loans to pay his armies. He was able to repay these loans with funds from his constituency. This became more difficult as time went on, and Frederick called for more stringent tax-collection efforts by his officials.

Correspondences in the register show how one of his loan arrangements worked. In 1239, Frederick had borrowed one thousand silver marks from Viennese merchant Heinrich Baum, who also provided housing in Vienna for Russian ambassadors on their way to the emperor in Cremona. Frederick acknowledged a debt of one thousand four hundred ounces of gold in January 1240, and knew he could not come up with that much cash. He proposed that Baum be allowed to export two large shiploads of grain from Apulia. This grain could be sent anywhere but Venice, now an enemy territory, and it would be exempt from taxes. The sale price would be 1,487 ounces of gold, repaying the debt with interest. Baum, who did not have much choice, agreed to the arrangement. This register also shows the workings of the grain deal cited in chapter 6, when Frederick closed grain markets to Genoese traders trying to gather grain to sell in North Africa, where there was a shortage.

The register also shows examples of Frederick's concerns on a local level. One letter relates the donation of one thousand cattle to the Muslim community of Lucera. This was to bind the residents there to the soil, and to try to increase the supply of the pack animals that were the transportation system of any medieval army. The justiciar of western Sicily reached accord regarding the numbers of pack animals to be furnished by Lucera in late 1239, which was approved by Frederick in this correspondence. Frederick thought he would lose the Muslims' agricultural expertise by isolating them in Lucera, where they were employed in stockkeeping and military manufacture. His solution was to import more Jews from Arabic lands. There is correspondence during this time about where and how the Jews would be settled. Even at the height of his dispute with the pope, Frederick continued to follow the customary practice of confining Jews to certain areas and forbidding them from building new synagogues. An increase of Jews in the kingdom meant an increase in receipts from the poll tax and other kinds of taxes, which was welcome as well.

The extent of Frederick's concern with day-to-day economic realities is unusual among medieval monarchs. Part of this is due to his absence from the kingdom, as reports that may have been made orally with a resident monarch had to be done in written form to an absent monarch. Certainly the need to finance his conflicts should have been motivation enough for him to keep up with such matters, but other rulers during this time did not attend to business in such a meticulous way. The result was that the kingdom paid for his vast effort against the pope and the Lombards, even though it was a small part of Frederick's realms. This took a large toll on the kingdom, which became somewhat depopulated and financially exhausted by the time of Frederick's death. The long-term effects for southern Italy and Sicily would show up under Frederick's successors.

Government business was not the only topic of these correspondences. Frederick was still emperor, and he intended to live like one. The letters contain instructions on such topics as getting slaves to serve in his private band, and what instruments they should play. There was comment on the securing and disposition of camels from North Africa. One letter asks for particular types of wines and foods to be sent to his camp, and there is correspondence with Master Theodore about medicines needed by the court.

The construction of new buildings was mostly on hold because of the expense being incurred by the military. However, the repair of existing castles had to continue. There is correspondence with the castellans and the local justiciars about this process. Frederick allowed the continuation of construction on his two favorite buildings: the Gate of Capua and the Castel del Monte. Frederick limited this expense, but construction did not totally stop.

One of the sources states that more than a third of the letters addressed hunting.[2] Falcons were a major topic, with the emperor expressing his wish to hunt more often. He kept up with his supply of falcons from all over, and the status of falcons that were left in the kingdom. Frederick asked that six hunting leopards, with their Muslim handlers, be sent to him, first in Pisa, then later on his progress south. When Frederick was on campaign, hunting was his main form of recreation. As we have seen, Frederick had a hard time getting his opponents to meet him in open battle, so the main form of warfare involved sieges. By their nature, sieges are stationary, and if the commander wishes, he can take time off from the day-to-day details. This cost Frederick greatly in a later siege, but before 1241, his propensity to indulge in hunting never caused him any trouble.

This ability to take time off while on campaign was important, as Frederick or his subordinates were on campaign during much of his reign. (The normal practice in medieval times was to campaign in a seasonal manner, marching and fighting only in the summer and autumn.) At any given time, there was some kind of conflict going on in Frederick's domains, from northern Germany to the island of Sicily. Often he was not present for these fights, and he had to delegate the leadership of smaller armies.

One person he came to trust completely was his son Enzio, who became an important general, often operating independently. Enzio had already returned Frederick's birthplace, Jesi, to the kingdom from control of the Papal States, and he operated independently in northern and eastern Italy for quite a few years. Enzio's military career ended with his capture at Fossalta

2. Abulafia, *Frederick II: A Medieval Emperor*, 267.

by the forces of Bologna in 1249, which led to his imprisonment. Enzio remained a prisoner in Bologna until his death in
1270, but he was given the freedom of the city during the day,
returning to prison at dusk. He thus became a favorite of the
ladies of Bologna, and he composed love poems of high quality. Several poems dealing with his status as prisoner were also
attributed to him.

Frederick also trusted Ezzelino da Romano for the rest of his
life. Ezzelino was an effective soldier who mostly operated in
northeastern Italy. Ezzelino and Enzio often worked together.
Ezzelino's reputation as a cruel tyrant did not put Frederick off.
Ezzelino was always involved in a feud with the d'Este family
over territory in northeast Italy. He remained loyal to the
Hohenstaufen cause, even after Frederick died. Ezzelino was
destroyed by a papal army, after a crusade was declared against
him, in 1254.

Frederick had other military leaders, but most of the time
when something important was at stake on a campaign,
Frederick led it himself. Much of the propaganda issued by the
imperial court built up the emperor as a great military figure.
This evaluation was taken at face value by historians until the
twentieth century. Now, Frederick is viewed in a new light as a
soldier. T.C. Van Cleve says frankly that "any analysis of
Frederick as a military leader could result only in an unfavor-
able judgment."[3] I agree.

Frederick's biggest problem was coming to grips with fortified towns. His main conflicts were with the towns of the
Lombard League. All those towns were fortified, and Frederick
did not have a good record conducting sieges to a favorable
end. This was a problem for military commanders throughout

3. Van Cleve, *The Emperor Frederick II*, 535.

Europe at this time. Few battles were conducted on open ground. One such battle had been decisive for Frederick. The Battle of Bouvines destroyed the power of Otto IV and allowed Frederick's takeover of the empire. The lesson learned from that battle was to not leave walled cities if possible. Frederick's only real success as a general was Cortenuova, which was a good plan well–executed but was not decisive because the defeated army retreated to Milan, which could never be captured.

Still, Frederick was not often beaten (although in the next chapter we will look at his most devastating defeat). Most of his campaigns ended with small gains or losses, or stalemates. His main military purpose was to obtain the submission of all the Lombard towns, which he never achieved. Frederick was ahead of many of his contemporaries in one important military skill: administration. European armies of this time mostly consisted of two parts: the feudal troops, which were raised by nobles of the land, and mercenaries. The feudal troops were paid for by the noble initially, but if they stayed on campaign for awhile, the higher ruler (king or emperor) had to pick up the expenses. The mercenaries always fought for pay. The ability to keep armies in the field for a long time depended on finances. Frederick had learned the hard way, on his initial trip to Germany when he had little income, the importance of having the money to pay his troops. The correspondence that survives from 1239–40 is full of references to raising money to be sent to the emperor to pay his troops. Frederick was more successful than other rulers of this time in keeping up with these payments. Frederick subsidized the crusade in 1228, as discussed earlier.

There are no instances in the sources I reviewed in which Frederick's troops sacked a city without his permission. He ordered cities destroyed a few times, such as Sora, to make a political point. There are no examples of his unpaid troops becoming destructive looking for loot, which happened many times in medieval Europe. Frederick had the intelligence to use his Muslim subjects in units of their own, which were very effective militarily. The units were probably most effective psychologically against Christian opponents, who feared all Muslims.

There is little evidence that Frederick was an inspiring leader of his troops. The only example of his rallying forces by personal leadership came in Constance in 1212, when he persuaded the citizens to fortify the bridge that his opponent, Otto, needed to get to the city. Frederick did not have the common touch. His grandfather, Barbarossa, had it, and showed it as a fine military leader. Frederick did have presence, however. We have seen how, in Germany in 1212, in the kingdom in 1220, and on his return from crusade, his presence turned around a bad situation. This was mostly because of his reputation; in these instances, little fighting was involved.

The other campaign Frederick led to a successful conclusion was the crusade in 1228–29. He was able to put together a sizable army and keep it together for awhile in the face of condemnation of the pope, which was no mean feat. However, he achieved his goal on the crusade through diplomacy. That was a continual theme throughout Frederick's campaigns: he did not try to destroy the other parties but to force them into a settlement. Negotiations were always being conducted while he was on campaign.

This played into Frederick's strength. He was not a great soldier, but he was a very good diplomat. He could usually reach his goals through talking, after showing he was serious by exhibiting military force. He was able to get several truces in his conflicts with the pope and the Lombards. These would last until one party felt things were going badly, and the conflict would start up again. Although Frederick was able to forge lasting agreements with other powers in Europe and in the Holy Land, he could never do so with the Lombards or the pope. Because he could not militarily conquer the Lombards, and the pope was not a military target, these conflicts were in stalemate at Frederick's death.

Frederick was not much better or worse than his European contemporaries as a military leader. For instance, he utilized the heavy cavalry that was prominent in Europe at the time. There was a military genius operating during Frederick's lifetime, however, who did impinge on Central Europe using a different tactic: the Mongol Genghis Khan. The land empire he and his successors created was the largest ever seen on Earth, and it was conquered using light cavalry. The Mongols were always outnumbered on their campaigns against China, the Khwarezmian Empire (which consisted of modern Iran, Turkmenistan, and most of modern Uzbekistan and Afghanistan), and in eastern Europe. For a long time, opponents were foolish enough to meet the Mongols in open battle, invariably to the Mongols' advantage. Later opponents learned to hole up in fortified cities. The Mongols, after much frustration, learned to use captured military engineers to build siege engines that would either batter or terrify the cities into submission. Thus the Mongols were able to conquer much tougher opponents than were European armies of the time. The Mongols had entered Europe in the 1220s, getting to Hungary before leaving to return for the election of a new khan. Their devastation of Russia in the 1240s was such that they were able to rule Russia for the next 240 years. Frederick and other rulers of Europe were worried about a possible Mongol invasion of Europe, but it never happened in a full-scale manner. Whenever the Mongols encountered European armies, the Mongols rode circles around the heavy European cavalry and defeated them. Internal Mongol political developments kept them from continuing on to conquer Europe.

Frederick was known as a fine horseman and tried his best to keep his cavalry supplied with good mounts. He was taught the use of the various weapons of the time as a child, in the normal noble tradition. It is not known if he ever had to use the weapons as an active participant in one of his battles. Frederick was usually in good health, even with his continual travel on his campaigns. However, he was forty-seven in 1241, and that was past middle age in a time when the normal life span was about thirty. Political events conspired to keep him on campaign for most of the rest of his life.

TEN

Closing Years

WHEN POPE GREGORY IX DIED IN 1241, Frederick was on the verge of going to Germany to deal with the Mongol threat to the empire. He chose not to go, feeling that the opportunity to influence the selection of a new pope was more important. He left his son Conrad to deal with the Mongol threat. Conrad issued orders to gather an army, but because he was only thirteen, the actual gathering of the army and the campaign were in the hands of the princes of the empire in Germany. They met the Mongols at Liegnitz. The imperial army was defeated, and the way was open for the Mongols to add Central Europe to their empire. The only thing that stopped them was the death of their great khan back in Mongolia, which meant all the leaders had to return there to elect a new leader. So the Mongol army left Central Europe, saving the empire and changing the course of history.

A NEW POPE

The selection of a new pope in medieval times always depended on local political conditions in Rome (or later, in Avignon). This process was not the dignified process we see in modern times. In 1241, there were two main political conditions to deal with.

One was the presence of the emperor nearby and his holding of two cardinals who were eligible to participate in the election. The cardinals, James of Palestrina and Nicholas of Ostia, were opponents of Frederick's, and their having been prisoners of his for the last few months did not make them more amenable to Frederick's wishes.

The other political situation was the rivalry between the two most powerful families in Rome, the Orsini and the Colonna. Frederick had captured Cardinal Giovanni Colonna along with other churchmen trying to attend the council Pope Gregory had called. Frederick had turned his charm on Colonna, and the cardinal was now a strong supporter of Frederick's. The emperor had released Colonna, and he was in attendance at the start of the conclave to pick Gregory's successor. This factor in Frederick's favor was offset by the fact that Matteo Orsini was the senator of Rome, which meant he was effectively secular ruler of Rome. Orsini wanted the conclave to meet and quickly select a new pope who was antiemperor. To make this happen, Orsini confined the cardinals to a ramshackle palace in Rome, the Septizonium.

The Septizonium became a prison for the ten cardinals at the conclave, who were now living in conditions as bad as those experienced by the two cardinals Frederick held. The Septizonium was guarded by troops who used the roof as a lavatory. When it rained, the roof leaked, with predictable results for the cardinals, who were not allowed to leave for any reason. The basic division among the cardinals was six pro-

Frederick, four anti-Frederick. Soon, English Cardinal Robert of Somercote died because of the terrible conditions, changing the numbers to five against four. Eventually a compromise candidate was chosen, Cardinal Godfrey Castiglione, who took the name Celestine IV. Celestine was elected in October 1241, but the effect of the conclave was too much for this elderly man, who was acceptable to the emperor and Orsini. After a term of seventeen days, during which his only memorable action was to excommunicate Matteo Orsini, Celestine died.

Pope Innocent IV, the most consistent papal opponent of Frederick II. (*Syracuse University Library*)

During his term, some of the remaining cardinals had fled Rome to the town of Anagni. Cardinal Colonna remained in Rome, a prisoner of Orsini's. One other cardinal, Sinibaldo de'Fieschi, remained in Rome, as he was sympathetic to Orsini. The rest of the cardinals opened negotiations with Frederick to release the cardinals he was holding. Frederick wanted Gregorio di Montelongo recalled as papal representative in Lombardy. These negotiations went on for over a year and a half. During this time, the other rulers of western Christendom became more upset over the lack of a pope. The role of Matteo Orsini in imprisoning and intimidating the cardinals was forgotten, and Frederick became the main cause of the deadlock. Frederick eventually gave in, and in spring 1243, he released the cardinals he was holding. This resulted in the election, on June 25, 1243, of Sinibaldo de'Fieschi, who took the name Pope Innocent IV.

Innocent IV was a member of a Genoese noble family that was in the habit of sending younger sons into the church. He had been a canon lawyer and long-time associate of Gregory IX's. His family was thought to be Ghibelline in sympathy. This family had not helped Frederick when his forces were trying to take Genoa in 1241, being aware that their holdings were in jeopardy if Frederick took control of the area.

Frederick's initial reaction was favorable to Innocent's election. He sent an embassy of four of his highest officials, led by Piero della Vigna, to negotiate an end to Frederick's excommunication with the new pope. Innocent initially refused to meet this delegation, claiming he could not negotiate with an excommunicate or his representatives. This is when Frederick uttered his famous statement, "No pope can be a Ghibelline."[1] Frederick meant that even if a pope had supported the emperor prior to election, once he was elected pope, he could not continue as a supporter of the emperor's. Eventually, Innocent accepted the delegation and negotiations began.

In the meantime, a new development led to changes in the positions of both parties. Frederick had held the town of Viterbo in the Patrimony of St. Peter since 1240. Cardinal Rainer of Viterbo was Frederick's most determined opponent in the Curia. Rainer's intrigues in his hometown led to a coup d'etat in Viterbo in July 1243. This event confined a small imperial force to the citadel in town, while the Guelf families took control of the town. Frederick sent an army to try to take the town back and spent September through November 1243 besieging Viterbo. By November, Frederick felt the siege was not going to succeed. He opened negotiations to get his troops released from the citadel in exchange for lifting the siege. This

1. *The Emperor Frederick II*, 455.

was done through the pope, who promised safe conduct for the imperial troops. Pope Innocent sent Cardinal Otto of St. Nicholas, a supporter of Frederick's, to escort the troops from the citadel to Frederick's army. Cardinal Rainer led a contingent of Viterbo citizens in an attack on the imperial troops, and they massacred a good portion of them before they got to the imperial camp. This was done in the presence of Cardinal Otto, who reported it to the pope. The pope acted displeased and called on the citizens of Viterbo to make reparation to their Ghibelline opponents in town. Led by Cardinal Rainer, the Guelf citizens refused, and called the pope's bluff. This entire action put a damper on negotiations between the pope and the emperor.

The negotiations started up again in early 1244, and continued in Rome. An agreement was announced during Easter week at a grand conference of all the involved parties. The agreement was to turn back the clock on territorial matters in Italy to Palm Sunday 1239, the date of Frederick's latest excommunication. The pope had several spiritual conditions, to which Frederick agreed. Frederick was to support military action against the Mongols, which turned out not to be necessary. He was to aid King Louis IX of France on his crusade. Even though it appears Frederick may have come out second in these negotiations, he announced this agreement to his princes in Germany. He intended to meet face-to-face with Pope Innocent IV at Narni, about fifty miles north of Rome in the Papal States, in June 1244, to finalize and sign the agreement. Frederick got to Narni and met a representative of the pope's. Innocent had more conditions to impose regarding Lombardy. Frederick was not happy, but he felt he could charm the pope at a personal meeting to finalize matters.

FREDERICK IS DEPOSED

Pope Innocent IV started off for Narni but appears to have decided never to meet with the emperor. In a well-executed escape from his meeting with Frederick, he secretly went to the port of Civitavecchia, about thirty-five miles northwest of Rome. There he was picked up by a Genoese galley and taken to his hometown. He was hailed by his fellow Genoese. Innocent stayed three months because of illness, then intended to go to France to put more pressure on Louis to support him. However, Louis did not allow the pope to enter French territory, steering him to the town of Lyons. Even though Lyons was nominally part of the empire, Innocent felt secure enough there in December 1244 to issue a call for a general council of the church to meet in Lyons in June 1245. The subject of the council would be the status of the emperor.

Innocent seems to have thought he could not handle Frederick one-on-one. He believed Frederick would either charm him (as Frederick had done with Gregory in 1230), or ask for contrition in such a way that could not be turned down (as Emperor Henry IV had done with Pope Gregory VII at Canossa in 1076). Innocent now made up his mind that opposition to Frederick was more important to the church than Louis's crusade or opposition to the Mongols. When word of Innocent's escape reached Frederick, he still insisted that the Easter week agreement should apply. Frederick sent word that he would consider going on crusade again, as well as other actions the pope was considering. At the same time, Frederick was consolidating his control in central Italy, which, like northern Italy, was divided into towns with Guelf and Ghibelline factions. These local rivalries became more important in each particular town than any conflict between the pope and emperor. The continuation of these local conflicts drew in both the pope and emperor, and made peace unlikely.

In fact, the attitude of Pope Innocent IV and the Curia made peace impossible. The call for the council made it explicit that its main concern would be the status of the emperor. The propaganda war against Frederick was ratcheted up, with Cardinal Rainer contributing screeds calling Frederick everything negative he and his aides could think of, including fourth beast in the vision of the prophet Daniel, destroyer and devourer, new Herod, Sadducee, false crusader, friend of Muslims and Jews, enemy of Christian belief, capturer of cardinals, and usurper of papal lands and rights.

Frederick did not turn up the rhetorical heat at this time, but lay low under this provocation. He sent his leading legal mind, Taddeo da Suessa, to the council as his representative. The Council of Lyons opened on June 25, 1245. On June 28, Pope Innocent IV spoke on the topic of the emperor using the words of Jeremiah, "Behold, and see if there be any sorrow like unto my sorrow." He then ran through the normal litany of papal charges against Frederick. The only new one was that Frederick was a sodomite. The rest were the old favorites: church problems in Sicily, treatment of Muslims, treatment of the Lombard communes, Frederick's immorality, etc. The representatives at the council were mainly Italian, French, and Spanish. German clerics did not attend, showing again the continuing loyalty Frederick inspired in Germany.

As he was intimately familiar with these charges, Taddeo da Suessa had already prepared a reply that was coherent and cogently argued. He stressed that Frederick wished to comply with the Rome agreement, and gain absolution in the process. Taddeo stressed that the emperor was compliant, contrite, and willing to cooperate with the pope. He also said Frederick would act against the three enemies in eastern Europe: the Mongols, the Turks, and the current holders of Constantinople.

The main point of this presentation was to show that the emperor was willing to talk, and back up the talk with action. He also wanted to show that it was the pope who was unwilling to negotiate, and that the charges against the emperor were too serious to be considered without the emperor's own input. Pope Innocent claimed that these were fine words, but asked who could guarantee the emperor's compliance. Taddeo proposed that King Louis of France and King Henry of England would be suitable guarantors.

Innocent was in a bit of a bind. He knew that if Frederick appeared and was properly contrite in front of the council, it would be hard to deny him absolution. That would be a major propaganda victory for the emperor. Frederick was already moving through the Piedmont region toward Lyons in the summer of 1245. It seems that at this point, the pope made the final decision that there would be no negotiations with the emperor. Even though Taddeo's presentation had made many friends in the council, the pope did not accept any of it. At stake was the pope's authority to judge all mankind (which really meant all Catholics). On July 17, 1245, Pope Innocent IV pronounced sentence on Frederick. Stressing the emperor's immorality in his personal life and treatment of the captive cardinals, Innocent declared Frederick deposed from all thrones and stripped of all titles. Innocent took this action as pope, not on behalf of the council. Such an action had been taken before, by Pope Innocent III against Emperor Otto IV in Frederick's childhood. At that time, Frederick was the beneficiary.

Now the question was what effect the pope's declaration would have on the other crowned heads of Europe. Would they support the pope against a crowned brother? There was no way for the pope to enforce his declaration without their help. The German princes were a possible source of help, but they had elected Frederick originally and had remained loyal for over thirty years. The main effect of this deposition was that the pope declared an end to negotiations. It was now war to the end against the emperor and, in the normal medieval way, against his entire Hohenstaufen family. Pope Innocent IV characterized the Hohenstaufen as "a race of vipers."[2]

THE WHEEL OF FORTUNE

Frederick had been steadily moving toward Lyons during this time. He had called an imperial diet at Verona for spring of 1245, to meet with the princes of the empire. Many princes from Germany attended, led by Frederick's son Conrad. A proposal for Frederick to marry the heiress of the duke of Austria had been discussed via correspondence prior to the diet. The duke was willing, but his daughter, Gertrude, was not, having been influenced by the stories of Frederick's immorality. This was Frederick's last meeting with Conrad. They had a good relationship, so it seems Frederick learned from the mistakes he made with his first son, Henry.

After the diet concluded, Frederick continued moving toward Lyons. He was in Turin when word reached him of the decree of deposition by the pope at the Council of Lyons. Frederick called his court together, put on the imperial crown, and stated: "I have not yet lost my crown, neither will pope or council take it from me without a bloody war."[3] Frederick saw clearly that the pope was taking a step toward becoming temporal overlord of all Catholic kings, and he made his opposition clear. Frederick had long felt that the church should be overlord of all spiritual matters but had no place in day-to-day

2. Maurice Keen, *The Pelican History of Medieval Europe* (London, 1982), 173.
3. Masson, *Frederick II of Hohenstaufen*, 333.

affairs. He had admired and helped St. Francis of Assisi, and felt that the poverty and spirituality of the Franciscans should be the guide for the entire church. Frederick consistently opposed the efforts of Popes Innocent III, Honorius III, Gregory IX, and now Innocent IV to assert the temporal power of the church.

King Louis IX of France was the most important figure calling for peace between the pope and emperor. Louis was a committed crusader who intended to leave as soon as he could to fight in Egypt. He knew that the preaching of the pope in the neighborhood of France would take possible troops away from his expedition. Louis was persuaded by Frederick's arguments against the temporal power of the pope, and he tried to bring together the two parties. In 1246, Frederick submitted to an examination of faith by several prelates from his own realm. These parties submitted to Louis their findings that Frederick was an orthodox Roman Catholic. They then attempted to submit these finding to the pope. Louis urged Innocent to accept the findings so Louis could proceed effectively with his crusade. However, Pope Innocent declined to accept the findings and stated that only he could rule on Frederick's faith. He also said Frederick had to come to him alone and submit to an examination. After all that had happened, Frederick would never submit to those conditions.

How could the papacy enforce its decree of deposition? Frederick was king of Sicily and Holy Roman emperor, and he had many supporters in Lombardy and the Papal States. Some of the political extremists in the Curia wanted to call for a crusade against the emperor. Innocent, while willing to go far, would not go that far. The theory was accepted within the Curia that the now-deposed emperor was an illegitimate ruler who was a tyrant. Some canon lawyers argued that tyrannicide was acceptable. Many people in the kingdom were upset with the heavy taxation there, and the increasing economic control Frederick exerted over his domain caused unrest. The Curia hoped this was fertile ground for decisive action.

A conspiracy against Frederick's life was discovered in early 1246. Frederick was informed of the conspiracy while in Tuscany, on his way south to the kingdom. His informant was the count of Caserta, who was married to Frederick's illegitimate daughter Violante. At the same time Frederick was informed, word of their exposure reached two of the conspirators at court, who fled to Rome, where they were protected by papal representatives. The leader of the conspiracy was Bernardo Orlando Rossi, an old confidant of the emperor's who was also the pope's brother-in-law. Frederick learned of other conspirators in his various Italian realms. All who were caught suffered death. Their bodies were sent around to various towns in the kingdom to remind his subjects the fate that awaited traitors.

Understandably, Frederick felt that this conspiracy had been hatched at the highest levels of the Curia. Several of the conspirators had been captured while in the company of Minorite brothers, who had been preaching against the emperor. The reaction of the pope to the uncovering of the conspiracy was also revealing. He protected any conspirators who reached his representatives, and correspondence revealed that Innocent at least wished for the success of the conspiracy. There is no evidence that Innocent initiated the conspiracy, but that did not keep Frederick from escalating the war of words. He wrote his former brother-in-law, King Henry III of England, that Innocent was behind the conspiracy, without charging him formally.

There was unrest in all parts of Frederick's domain as a result of this conflict. Frederick spent the rest of 1246 in the kingdom, putting down the rebellions that had arisen. The church was aggressive in preaching against Frederick in Germany and Lombardy.

In Germany, not many were converted to fighting against the emperor who had ruled since 1212. But there was a small faction that opposed Frederick, led by the old regent, Henry Raspe of Thuringia. Henry Raspe was elected emperor by papal-adherent electors in 1246, and he even defeated Conrad in a battle at Frankfurt in 1246. But Raspe died in 1247, and opposition to Frederick died with him. Frederick had been planning to go to Germany to deal with the rebellion, but after Raspe died, the trip was unnecessary. Raspe's lands fell to the margrave of Meissen, who was married to Frederick's legitimate daughter Margaret. The great princes of Germany had not joined the rebellion, and Frederick's loose rule was preferred to any alternative.

The one great German prince who had opposed Frederick for a long time, Frederick Babenburg of Austria, had died in 1246. Frederick took over direct rule of this duchy and appointed his grandson Frederick (son of his deceased eldest son, Henry) to rule there. The church continued to try to incite opposition to Frederick in the parts of the empire north and west of the Alps, and its lack of success shows the effectiveness of Frederick's rule. Even in Burgundy, where Lyons was located, the papacy could not raise substantial forces to oppose the emperor.

As ever, Lombardy was a different story. Frederick had been in good shape in northern and central Italy at the time of the deposition. He had left military matters in these areas to Ezzelino and to his son Enzio when he returned to the kingdom in 1246. Frederick gained other adherents when his illegitimate son Manfred married Beatrice of Savoy. This led several lords in northwestern Italy to come over to the emperor's side. Pope

Innocent had raised some troops in the Lyons area and turned them over to Cardinal Ottaviano degli Ubaldini, a Tuscan prelate from a great landholding family who considered himself a military leader. However, the changing of sides by rulers in Savoy kept the cardinal's forces confined to Burgundy, because the duke of Savoy blocked the mountain passes between Burgundy and Lombardy, so these troops had no effect in 1247.

The Wheel of Fortune, a favorite medieval metaphor for the vagaries of life, had Frederick in a very good position in early summer 1247. The process of turning the wheel upside down started when papal forces, led by Frederick's enemies Gregorio di Montelongo and Bernardo Orlando Rossi, avoided Enzio's forces and took over the town of Parma in central Lombardy. Intrigue led by Gregorio had prepared the ground, and now Parma threw off allegiance to the emperor. Frederick felt that Parma's location astride access to the Arno valley and Tuscany from Lombardy was too valuable to let it fall to Guelf forces. Consequently, he changed his plans to go to Germany and brought the forces he had gathered to lay siege to Parma. Frederick arrived there in late summer 1247, and settled down for the siege.

Gregorio di Montelongo was the leader of Parma's defense for the entire siege. He granted crusader status to the defenders of Parma, meaning the soldiers were absolved of their sins. He turned out to be an effective leader, using all the stratagems and ruses at his disposal to keep up the morale of the defenders. Once, while Gregorio was hosting a dinner with the civic leaders of Parma, a dusty messenger arrived with a note that said the armies of the pope were on the way and would be there soon. This encouraged the Parma leaders, but it was all an act. The messenger was a servant of Gregorio's, and Gregorio had written the note.

The Guelf leaders of Mantua and Ferrara succeeded in bringing some supplies to Parma in early November. There were
papal forces at Mantua that were meant to come to the rescue
of Parma. Their leader, Cardinal Ottaviano, failed again in his
military mission, and those troops never appeared. The cardinal was accused of cooperating with Frederick, but he was able
to prove he was not in league with him.

When it became clear to Frederick in early autumn 1247 that
the siege of Parma would be a long one, he made his camp in a
unique way. Frederick ordered the construction of a town,
named Victoria, within sight of Parma, and he made clear that
Victoria would replace Parma after its destruction. Victoria was
designed to be a real town, with a cathedral and palace. All the
permanent construction was to be done in the future. As of
now, Victoria was a camp. Frederick put his court treasury,
library, traveling harem, and animal menagerie in Victoria. The
imperial army was camped there with all its supporting accoutrements, and it must have been quite a sight.

The siege of Parma continued until February 1248. Both
sides continued to observe the other and look for any break
that could change the status quo. The break came when
Frederick indulged in his passion for hunting. The Parmesans
learned that Frederick had gone on a hunting expedition in the
middle of February. They sent a sortie out of Parma, which
drew the remaining garrison out of Victoria. The rest of the
forces of Parma, joined by most of the residents, rushed the
short distance to Victoria and overwhelmed the garrison. The
hungry Parmesan troops and civilians first ate the food they
found in Victoria. Then the imperial camp was sacked and its
treasury taken. The Muslim members of the harem were taken
away. The imperial crown was captured and exhibited in
Parma's cathedral. The library was looted. One result was the

loss of Frederick's own copy of *De arte venandi cum avibus*. Fortunately, this manuscript eventually came into the possession of a citizen of Milan, who offered it to Charles of Anjou in 1264. The worst personal loss to Frederick was the capture of Taddeo di Suessa, one of his longest-serving and most loyal servants. Taddeo's hands were amputated, then he was imprisoned and executed.

Frederick learned of this disaster from messengers while on the hunt. He and his companions returned to Victoria, but too late. He decided there was nothing he could do at that moment, and led his remaining forces to Cremona. (This involved Frederick's staying in the saddle for twenty-four straight hours, which speaks well of his physical condition at the advanced age, for medieval times, of fifty-three.) Victoria was the worst military defeat Frederick suffered in his career. He returned to Parma with the army he could gather three days later, and Enzio captured supply ships intended for Parma. This capture resulted in three hundred prisoners being taken; all were executed. In a later battle in the area, Frederick's forces, led by Manfred Lancia, defeated papal forces led by Bernardo Orlando Rossi. Manfred's forces cut Bernardo to pieces immediately after capturing him.

The Wheel of Fortune had turned upside down for Frederick. Even the successes after Victoria did not alter the fact that Frederick had suffered a major defeat. Frederick had to lick his wounds and restore his finances. This involved levying new taxes in the kingdom and appealing to his friends for help. The taxes were more severe than before, but the prior repression of rebellion kept the lid on. It appears Frederick got some financial help from his son-in-law, John Vatatzes, the Greek emperor. Frederick secured loans from Sienese bankers, mortgaging the silver mine of Montieri to get ready cash. Frederick remained in northern Italy but took no more military action during the rest of 1248. He sent many missives to his subordinates in the kingdom, concentrating on saving his base there.

The next couple of years saw the peak of papal success against Frederick. His old enemy Cardinal Rainer of Viterbo led papal troops to take Frederick's birthplace, Jesi. After that, Rainer retired from active duty because of old age (he died in early 1250) and was replaced by other leaders in central Italy. These papal delegates were successful in winning back territory in the Papal States until 1250. Meanwhile, Pope Innocent was preparing to invade the kingdom. He issued detailed edicts proclaiming all Frederick's laws invalid. While he was taking these political steps, he was attempting to gather troops for an invasion. The troops he gathered were effective in central Italy, but never were able to carry off a successful invasion because of the strength of opposition in the kingdom.

Frederick remained in northern Italy for the rest of 1248. He went to Piedmont for the marriage of his son Manfred, and remained in Cremona most of the rest of the year. Frederick was concerned with holding as much territory as he could in Lombardy and Piedmont against the machinations of the Lombard League. There were various defections of north Italian towns between Guelf and Ghibelline allegiance, but nothing vital to rouse Frederick to military action at this time. In the northern empire, a new opponent was raised up with the help of the pope—William of Holland, who declared his opposition to the emperor. It turned out that William did not have as much support as Henry Raspe had had and was mostly concerned with extending his duchy to include neighboring provinces. Frederick allowed Conrad to handle that problem, which was resolved on the battlefield. William submitted to Conrad and swore allegiance in 1250.

One major result of this constant conflict with the forces of
the pope was the continuing personal isolation of Frederick. He
became, as have many rulers throughout history, more suspicious of the motives of the people surrounding him as he
became older. The assassination attempt of a few years prior
accentuated this tendency. Frederick became more dependent
on the people he felt he could rely on. His main personal sup-
ports were his sons and sons-in-law. Even after his bad experience with his eldest son, Henry, Frederick had established all his
legitimate and illegitimate sons in responsible positions by this
time. Conrad had been left in Germany to rule since the early
1240s. Frederick's correspondences to Conrad indicate they
had a good relationship, even though they had not seen each
other since their last meeting in 1245. Enzio was a leading general in Frederick's army. Other sons were given domains in the
empire and the kingdom, and they ruled these areas under
Frederick's far-off supervision.

After the death of Taddeo di Suessa, Frederick's main subordinate in ruling the kingdom was Piero della Vigna. Piero had
been with Frederick since the early 1220s, aided in writing the
Constitutions of Melfi, and had long been a High Court justice.
In 1247, Frederick appointed Piero to the joint offices of
protonotary and logothete of the Kingdom of Sicily. This made
Piero the second-most-powerful person in the kingdom. He had
already been powerful for quite a while, and had taken advantage of that power to build up his fortune the way medieval government officials usually did—by taking a cut of the money that
passed through his hands. As Piero was not of noble birth, this
enrichment caused much resentment among the nobles of the
kingdom, who waited for the opportunity to bring him down.

Even with these enemies, Piero had been at Frederick's side
for over two decades. He had been trusted with delicate diplo-

matic missions, such as the negotiations arranging Frederick's marriage to Isabella of England. Piero had written many of Frederick's edicts and much of the correspondence condemning the papacy. He thought he was in a secure position. This changed after another assassination attempt on Frederick in late 1248. Chronicler Matthew Paris reported that a doctor at the court poisoned a drink intended for the emperor. Frederick learned about this and asked the doctor to drink first. The doctor knocked the drink over and claimed it was an accident. Supposedly, Frederick was able to save some of the liquid, and ordered a condemned criminal to drink the remaining portion. The criminal died, and the doctor was put to death. Although Piero was supposedly present during this episode, he was not immediately suspected and continued with his duties. Piero's enemies intimated to the emperor that Piero was aware of the poison in the drink.

In January 1249, in Cremona, Piero was suddenly seized and taken to prison. He was charged with embezzlement, treason, and plotting with the pope for Frederick's assassination. Piero was probably guilty of the first charge, but the others had little basis other than Frederick's growing suspicion of everyone around him. Piero was intentionally blinded while in prison, and a month later he committed suicide by bashing his head against the stone wall of his prison cell. This fate so impressed Dante that he included Piero in canto 13 of the *Inferno* with other famous suicides. In the poem, Piero does not say anything against the emperor, other than that Frederick was influenced by jealous courtiers against him. Piero proclaims his loyalty to Frederick for all eternity.

Another great problem arose for Frederick the following month. At a battle outside Fossalta, Bolognese forces captured

Frederick's son Enzio. Although Enzio had been culpable at the disaster of Parma, he had been an effective military leader for Frederick, and a thoroughly trusted companion. Frederick offered much for Enzio's release, but, as mentioned earlier, the Bolognese never freed him, and he remained a prisoner until he died in 1270.

After his attempts to free Enzio failed, Frederick withdrew to the kingdom in late 1249. This was the low point of his struggle with the pope and the Lombards. Frederick lost the allegiance of Como and Modena, and regained the allegiance of Ravenna during this time. Pope Innocent IV then made his first attempt to entice a high-born noble to lead an effort to replace Frederick in the kingdom, summoning Richard of Cornwall to Lyons. This was a strange choice, as Richard was the brother of the late Isabella of England, Frederick's dead wife. Richard had met and liked Frederick on Richard's way back from the Holy Land, and Richard knew the strength of Frederick's position in the kingdom. Richard listened to the pope, then declined the honor. This was only the beginning of a long papal search to replace the Hohenstaufen on the throne of the Kingdom of Sicily.

While Frederick remained in the kingdom in 1250, the military situation in all his domains brightened. Frederick had suffered ill health in 1249, and spent most of 1250 recovering. His military lieutenants in central Italy, Lombardy, and Germany all scored victories that turned the Wheel of Fortune in Frederick's favor. In central Italy, Walter of Manupello led forces from the kingdom to take control of the March of Ancona, the duchy of Spoleto, and Romagna. In Lombardy, Frederick's troops were led by Hubert Pallavicini, who scored a victory against the army of Parma in August. This resulted in the capture of more than one thousand prisoners. Hubert was known for his cruelty against prisoners, and he indulged in this cruelty while executing all those captured from the battle. In Germany, Conrad led a force into the lower Rhine Valley and defeated William of Holland. Conrad signed an armistice with William, ending his rebellion and confirming Conrad as overseer of German affairs.

These victories on the imperial side caused consternation on the papal side. All the defeated forces clamored for money, which the pope supplied. This emptied the papal treasury and led Innocent to impose ever more demands for money on the churches in areas not controlled by Frederick, which was slow in coming. Furthermore, King Louis IX of France had gone on crusade to Egypt in late 1248, and in April 1250, he and his army were captured by the Egyptians. Louis was eventually released after payment of a large ransom. Louis then sent his brothers Charles and Alfonso, along with Henry of Burgundy, to Pope Innocent in late 1250 to insist that he make peace with the emperor. Many European nobles blamed the pope for the failure of Louis's crusade, and Innocent was so uncertain of his position in Lyons that he asked King Henry of England about sanctuary there. Even after these reverses, and after the opprobrium Innocent was receiving regarding the failed crusade, the pope would not negotiate with the emperor. He stated this to a group of Tuscan nobles on December 7, 1250.

THE DEATH OF FREDERICK

By December 1250, Frederick had recovered his health and political position. He had spent the year in the kingdom, keeping up with the administration there and indulging in his love for hunting. He claimed he still was feeling good late in the year. However, while on the road in Capitanata in December, Frederick fell ill with dysentery. He was trying to get to his palace in Foggia when he died in the town of Fiorentino on December 13, 1250, less than two weeks short of his fifty-sixth birthday. He was attended by his favorite son, Manfred, and his lifelong friend and loyal prelate, Archbishop Berard of Palermo. The emperor was dressed in the robes of a Cistercian monk, and was shriven and made confession to Berard. A prophecy had been made years earlier that Frederick would die in a town named after flowers. Consequently, Frederick had always avoided Florence. As it happened, he died in Fiorentino, which is the name of a flower in Italian.

Manfred spread the word of his father's death throughout his realms. He wrote to his half-brother Conrad, "The sun of the world which illuminated mankind has set—the sun of justice has gone down; the author of peace has passed away."[4] The reaction from Pope Innocent IV was quite different: "Let heaven exult and the earth rejoice."[5] The papal chaplain, Nicholas of Carbio, gave vent to the high polemic generally used in this conflict by writing:

> At length God, from his sacred throne on high, seeing the bark of Peter floundering in the waves and being dashed to pieces by various oppressions and misfortunes, snatched away, in the midst of life, the tyrant and son of Satan, Frederick . . . Who died horribly, deposed and excommunicated, suffering excruciatingly from dysentery, gnashing his teeth, frothing at the mouth, and screaming, at the castle Fiorentino in Apulia, in the year of our Lord 1250.[6]

4. Abulafia, *Frederick II: A Medieval Emperor*, 407.

5. Van Cleve, *The Emperor Frederick II*, 529.

6. Van Cleve, *The Emperor Frederick II*, 529.

Frederick II. (*Vatican Library*)

ELEVEN

Legacy

A T HIS DEATH, FREDERICK II was able to accomplish one of
the main goals of any ruler. He was able to pass on his
realms, peacefully, to his legitimate sons. Frederick finalized his
will on December 7, 1250. In it, he named Conrad as his heir
to all realms in Germany, Italy, and Sicily. He named his other
legitimate son, Henry (son of Isabella of England), as ruler of
Arles or Jerusalem, at Conrad's choice, and successor to
Conrad if Conrad died without issue. Frederick also named his
illegitimate son Manfred as regent in the kingdom, in the
absence of Conrad. Manfred was his long-time favorite and
most-trusted son. He was entrusted with the emperor's intellectual legacy, the falconry book. Manfred fulfilled his mission of
keeping the manuscript together, and he made several additions
that are included in the current text.

Conrad was confirmed in his offices as Holy Roman emper-
or and king of Sicily soon after Frederick's death. The conflict

with the papacy continued, so there was no crowning of the emperor by the pope. Conrad stayed in the northern part of the empire, ruling there until his untimely death at age twenty-six in 1254. His half-brother Henry had died in 1252, so no legitimate sons of Frederick's remained. This was the end of Hohenstaufen rule of the empire. It was also the end of any claims of the emperor to universal rule. Emperors continued to be chosen by the electors of the Holy Roman Empire, until it was extinguished in 1806. The name of the empire was changed in the fifteenth century to the Holy Roman Empire of the German Nation.

Frederick II is not highly viewed in German history. He had shown the ability to create a strong state in the Kingdom of Sicily, but he did not attempt to do this in Germany. The process of state building was gaining speed in England, France, Aragon, Castile, Portugal, and the Kingdom of Sicily at this time, but Frederick accepted the political situation as he found it in Germany, as left by his grandfather Barbarossa and his father. Because Frederick had decided early on to concentrate on Italian affairs, he would have had a hard time following a different political course in Germany.

Frederick's accomplishment in Germany was maintaining the status quo. He was able to do this over a reign of thirty-eight years, while spending only nine of those years in Germany. The amazing accomplishment of mostly keeping the peace during this time has been downplayed in German histories. What has been stressed is the growth of power of the princes of the empire, leaving Germany behind in the nation-building race of western Europe. There is no doubt this is true, but it was a conscious decision by Frederick to get what he could out of Germany and concentrate on the Italian portion of his realms.

It was quite an accomplishment for a teenager who had been brought up in Sicily, without learning German, to go to Germany in 1212 and peacefully (for the most part) take over the northern part of the empire. Frederick remained popular in Germany, holding it in the empire throughout his reign and shrugging off rebellion at various times. The contretemps with his eldest son, Henry, was the main disappointment of his German reign. He learned from his mistakes with Henry, and his son Conrad became a successful ruler of Germany during Conrad's short life. After Frederick's death, a folk legend arose that he was not dead but was sleeping under a mountain castle at Kyffhäuser, awaiting the call to save Germany. This legend held until the fifteenth century, when it was transferred to his grandfather Barbarossa, a more congenial figure to the Germans of the time. A monument was built there to Barbarossa in 1896.

The main arena of Frederick's political activity was Italy. Frederick came closer to uniting it under one leader than anyone since the Roman Empire. Even so, he did not come very close. Frederick was able to impose strong rule on the Kingdom of Sicily. He was able to conquer and hold various parts of central and northern Italy. But he could never bring the Papal States nor the communes of the Lombard League under his effective control. There was a time early in his reign when Frederick would have accepted the Lombard communes to his rule under the same conditions as the princely states in Germany. That loose rule might have worked. But the Lombard communes had advanced beyond willingness to accept even that condition. Frederick spent the rest of his life futilely trying to impose rule on communes that would not accept it.

As we have seen, Frederick was good at many things. However, it has also been noted that he was not distinguished as a soldier. The inability to deal with fortified cities was his military downfall in his conflict with the Lombards. In this trait, Frederick had much in common with all European military leaders of his time. The effective way to deal with fortified cities was being developed at this time, but on the other side of the world, in a China that had many more fortified cities than Europe. These techniques, developed by the Mongols, did not make their way to Europe for a couple more centuries. Hence, no military solution to his Italian problems was achieved in Frederick's lifetime.

Frederick's other major conflict in Italy was with the papacy. During his adulthood, Frederick had to deal with four popes. He had reasonable relations with the first two, Innocent III and Honorius III. The conflict between Frederick and the final two, Gregory IX and Innocent IV, dominated the last twenty-four years of his life. Frederick and Gregory achieved a truce from 1230 until the second excommunication in 1239, but no peace was achieved for the rest of Frederick's life. The main contention was always the temporal power of the papacy. We in the modern world are used to the pope having no temporal power. That had been true in the history of the papacy until Innocent III. However, his assertion of rule over all rulers from the Donation of Constantine inevitably led to a break with leaders, and Frederick was the first one to feel the effects.

In the Kingdom of Sicily after Frederick's death, Manfred had been appointed regent in Conrad's absence. Conrad never returned to the kingdom before his own death, so, on Conrad's death, Manfred claimed the crown. He originally negotiated with Pope Innocent IV for recognition and was granted a meeting in Naples in 1254. On arriving in Naples, Innocent issued laws reorganizing Sicily more in the manner of the Lombard communes than Frederick's kingdom. This meant making the towns of the kingdom free communes, and dismantling of the centralized Sicilian bureaucracy. Manfred did not even quarrel with the pope, but withdrew to the Muslim stronghold of Lucera. He then denounced the pope's interference in kingdom affairs and called the Sicilian nobility together to secure their approval for his assumption of the throne.

This approval was attained in late 1254, after the death of Innocent IV. This process had been followed in the kingdom in 1130 and 1190, and would be again in 1282. It had also been followed on the death of Manfred's grandfather, Henry VI. At that time the bastard Tancred had been elected, so the election of someone with Manfred's legal status was not unprecedented.

Manfred reestablished the effective rule of the king of Sicily. He was uncontested in the kingdom and was able to keep peace with the new pope. This changed in the early 1260s, when Manfred responded to pleas from Ghibelline towns in Lombardy and Tuscany for help. Manfred got involved in the continual conflicts there, which led to a changed papal attitude. The pope at this time, Urban IV, continued the policy of Pope Innocent IV by trying to find a noble champion to militarily depose Manfred from the throne of the kingdom. This search had been going on in a sporadic manner since 1249. In 1262, Urban IV, a Frenchman, recruited Charles of Anjou, the brother of King Louis IX of France. Charles was kept on hold for a couple of years while Urban and Manfred negotiated, but before Urban's death in 1264, Charles and Urban reached agreement on Charles's expedition against the kingdom.

Charles did not rush to keep the agreement. He spent all of 1265 organizing his support, both military and political. Charles tried to raise money in France for the expedition but did not have much success. Most of his financial support came from the pope. His army gathered in the area of Rome in late

1265. Charles invaded the kingdom in early 1266, after being crowned king of Sicily by the pope. Manfred met Charles at the Battle of Benevento on February 26, 1266, and was killed in the fighting. Charles buried Manfred with respect, and Manfred retained a good reputation. Dante put him in Purgatory, even though Manfred had been in an excommunicated state when he died.

Charles of Anjou faced one more immediate threat from the Hohenstaufen. Emperor Conrad had left an infant son, born in 1253. The boy, Conradin, had been living in Germany since his father's death. Some north Italian Ghibellines called on him to come south, imitating in geographical reverse the journey of his grandfather Frederick. Conradin went south and was able raise a substantial treasury and army from Germany and northern Italy. He led an invasion of the kingdom in 1268, and met Charles in battle at Tagliacozzo in August. Charles won and eventually captured Conradin. He tried Conradin and any other Hohenstaufen progeny he could get his hands on, and then executed them in October 1268.

Charles thought he had ended the Hohenstaufen threat, and he was right—for a while. However, in a famous episode of Sicilian history, a spontaneous rising known as the Sicilian Vespers occurred in 1282. This popular rising, immortalized in a Verdi opera, resulted in the deaths of many of the French faction ruling the island. Various nobles in Sicily hoped to take advantage of the situation, and they dispatched an emissary to Manfred's daughter, Queen Constance of Aragon. Constance's husband, King Pedro of Aragon, had a long-standing dispute with Charles of Anjou over territories in North Africa. It was agreed that Pedro would sail, ostensibly for North Africa, but really for the island of Sicily. The nobles of Sicily gathered and asked Pedro to take over the crown, which he did in August

1282. Now the kingdom was divided between the mainland part, held by the Angevins, and the island of Sicily, held by the Aragonese. This was the reintroduction of the Hohenstaufen, in the female line, to the kingdom.

The history of the kingdom after this is a continual battle between the mainland and island portions, with one or the other taking total control at various times. Popes continued to try to influence the rulers there, always getting involved in determining the legitimacy of the kings of Sicily. The popes also continued to try to influence the rulers of the northern Italian communes, always supporting the Guelf faction and opposing the Ghibellines. This conflict lasted until the Guelfs extirpated the Ghibellines by eliminating all their power, which happened by the fifteenth century.

The conflict in northern Italy led Dante to write his short work *De Monarchia*. Dante argued that the papacy was not fit to rule the temporal affairs of men, though he fully agreed with the church's position of prominence in spiritual affairs. Dante argues in *De Monarchia* for a unification of Italy under the emperor. He makes the same point in the *Divine Comedy*. As there was no other power in the area, Dante felt that his desired unification could only be accomplished under the empire, and he wanted to see it happen. This was true even though Dante was of the White Guelf party in Florence, the Ghibellines of Florence having all been expelled in the late thirteenth century.

Dante also put various actors in the drama of Frederick's life in the *Divine Comedy*, many of whom I have cited. Charles of Anjou and Pedro of Aragon are joined in the same stanza of canto 7 of the *Purgatorio*, regarding negligent rulers. St. Francis of Assisi and Thomas Aquinas are joined in cantos 10 and 11 of the *Paradiso*, as examples of great Christians. Frederick's uncle, King William II of Sicily, is cited in canto 20 of the

Paradiso as an example of a just and temperate ruler. So where did Dante put Frederick? He is consigned, in the same stanza (canto 10 of the *Inferno*) as Cardinal Ottaviano degli Ubaldini, to the realm of the epicures. Frederick is mentioned many times in the poem, usually in a way that indicates that the Kingdom of Sicily was in better shape under him than it was under present—that is, early 1300s—rule.

Frederick's body was taken from Fiorentino to Palermo, where it was laid to rest in a porphyry coffin he had selected twenty years earlier. Frederick had requested a simple burial, but that request was not honored. A procession from Fiorentino through Apulia to Taranto allowed mainland subjects to pay their respects. The sea journey from Taranto took the body to Palermo. There an elaborate mass was said before the sarcophagus was placed in the Cathedral of Palermo beside the sarcophagus of his first wife, Constance, where it remains.

It is clear that Frederick would have been happy being buried in a consecrated area. Frederick considered himself to be a good Catholic. He was able to convince most of the clergy that served in areas he ruled of this, such as his old friend and companion Archbishop Berard of Palermo. Frederick participated in religious services throughout his life and felt that the spiritual side of life should be in the hands of the Roman Catholic Church. Frederick was a forerunner of the Reformation, along with many other Catholics of this time, in his condemnation of the power, wealth, and corruption of the church. He felt that a church organized more in the line of St. Francis of Assisi's teachings was necessary.

Another difference between Frederick and the church of this time was Frederick's treatment of other religions. Frederick respected other beliefs and did not try to convert the Muslims and Jews under his rule to Christianity. Frederick learned about those other religions and did not automatically assume that their adherents were going to hell because they did not believe in Christianity. It is true that Frederick's court was not as multicultural as his grandfather Roger II's in Sicily in the prior century, nor as Toledo in Castile of this time. But Frederick allowed much more open intellectual inquiry at his court than any other in Europe at the time. This did not change the fact that politically, he treated Muslims and Jews more in line with common contemporary European practice. They were tolerated but had to pay special taxes, and they could not spread their religions. Frederick did not have much trouble with Jews, even importing more to help agricultural matters in the kingdom. He had trouble with rebellious Muslims on the island of Sicily, which he solved in an innovative way (for the time) by concentrating them in Lucera. Until the sixteenth century, the normal solution to such a problem in Europe was expulsion. The Muslims of Lucera were expelled from the kingdom in 1300.

Frederick's conflict with the papacy was the salient fact of the last twenty-five years of his life. Frederick was able to hold his own throughout this conflict. Our modern view is that Frederick was on the correct side because we are used to separation of church and state. The attitude was different then. The papal exercise of temporal power that had effectively started with Innocent III continued until 1870. Temporal leaders, particularly in the Italian peninsula, had to continually deal with this fact. Frederick's warning to his fellow rulers came true.

Some writers have considered Frederick an early Renaissance figure. Others have called him the first modern man. Frederick was not confined to any one era, other than the one he lived in. His political aspirations went back to the ancient Roman Empire. He was open about this, showing it on the coins of the kingdom. Many of his statements show that he intended to rule as universal emperor. His military activities in northern Italy attempted to make his rule effective there, as it had been under ancient Rome.

Frederick foreshadowed the Renaissance in his patronage of the arts. Many of the princes of central and northern Italy followed his example by creating courts where the arts flourished. Frederick imported the Provençal practice of vernacular poetry, which helped to end the use of Latin as the main language of literature. All of the paintings and most of the sculptures created for his court have vanished, but it is known that Frederick commissioned many works of art. The buildings that remained from his constructions were available for emulation during the Renaissance, and many nobles copied their designs.

His scientific endeavors were ahead of his time. *De arte venandi cum avibus* was a manual for a hunter in the use of falcons and a record of a lifetime of ornithological observation. Frederick had studied the available literature on the subject, including Aristotle and other sources from the Arab world. He then compared it to what he saw and came down on the side of observation. This was a big step forward, shared in the later thirteenth century by English friar Roger Bacon. Both men were part of the change from total submission to existing texts to experimental science.

Frederick was not innovative in his political actions. The existing bureaucracy he found in place in both the empire and the kingdom when he became emperor were not changed substantially. Frederick improved and tightened control in the kingdom, but he was using the methods of his Norman predecessors. Frederick reached a higher state of centralization in the kingdom than existed anywhere else in Europe, but it was accomplished using contemporary practices. Frederick's cruelty to anyone who committed crimes against his person as either emperor or king was consistent with his times. Throughout his reign, Frederick continued to strive for order, and saw his role as the head of the political state as a means to preserve this order.

Frederick accomplished more than any other crusader of the thirteenth century. The crusading impulse of Europe had weakened since the great outpouring of the late eleventh century and the establishment of the crusader states in the Holy Land. Even popular movements led by legendary figures like Barbarossa and Richard the Lion-Hearted failed in the late twelfth century. Frederick was able to accomplish the goal of his crusade, the reacquisition of Jerusalem, through diplomatic means. For this he was condemned by the pope, even though the treaty he signed with al-Kamil held for the entire period of the agreement. Frederick's successful negotiations with the Muslims led ultimately to the pope declaring a crusade against Frederick.

Frederick's actions in northern and central Italy laid the foundation for the Renaissance. The political geography of the fifteenth and sixteenth centuries was established during the wars of the thirteenth century. The well-known political entities of Milan, Florence, Venice, Genoa, and others were strengthened during their conflicts with Frederick. Their independence was confirmed by their resistance to the power of the emperor. The leaders of these city-states also learned from Frederick and his subordinates like Ezzelino, as they became less democratic and more authoritarian in their rule.

While Frederick was not a Renaissance or modern figure, he was the most interesting European figure of his time. His wide-ranging interests, from astrology to ornithology, made him worthy of the designation *Stupor Mundi*. His constant conflict with the papacy foreshadowed the Reformation, and his interests in the arts and sciences foreshadowed the Renaissance. While he was not successful in eliminating the political power of the papacy, that struggle was a stalemate during his lifetime. He did the best he could to allow his descendants to continue the struggle. The fact that his sons were not able to succeed shows that the political system for such success had not yet been perfected. The conflict between secular leaders and the papacy continued for hundreds of years until the political power of the pope was virtually eliminated in the nineteenth century.

As for Frederick himself, his legend grew after his death. For the next century, people emerged in both the kingdom and the empire who claimed to be him or his reincarnation. Frederick had left behind a Germany ruled by the princes, which continued until the establishment of the Second Reich by Bismarck in 1870. The Kingdom of Sicily was under a new family of rulers after Manfred's death, but some of the people there who could remember the times of Frederick spread the story of a golden age. This belief shows the effect Frederick had on his time, and the reason for continued interest in Emperor Frederick II of Hohenstaufen.

BIBLIOGRAPHY

Abulafia, David. *Frederick II: A Medieval Emperor*. London: Allen Lane, 1988.

Alighieri, Dante. *Divine Comedy*. Translated by John Ciardi. New York: Norton, 1970.

Alighieri, Dante. *De Monarchia*. Translated by Herbert Schneider. New York: Houghton Mifflin, 1957.

Andrewes, Patience. *Frederick II of Hohenstaufen*. London: Oxford University Press, 1970.

Barber, Richard. *Henry Plantagenet, 1133-1189*. New York: Barnes & Noble, 1993.

Bishop, Morris. *The Middle Ages*. New York: Houghton Mifflin, 2001.

Cahill, Thomas. *Mysteries of the Middle Ages*. New York: Random House, 2006.

Cantor, Norman F. *The Civilization of the Middle Ages*. New York: Harper Collins, 1994.

Dahmus, Joseph. *A History of the Middle Ages*. New York: Barnes & Noble, 1995.

De Hartog, Leo. *Genghis Khan, Conqueror of the World*. New York: Barnes & Noble, 1999.

Einstein, David. *Emperor Frederick II*. New York: Philosophical Library of America, 1949.

Frederick II of Hohenstaufen. *The Art of Falconry*. Translated by Casey A. Wood and F. Marjorie Fyfe. Stanford: Stanford University Press, 1943.

Johnson, Paul. *Art: A New History*. New York: Harper Collins, 2003.

Jordan, William Chester. *Europe in the High Middle Ages*. London: Penguin, 2001.

Kantorowicz, Ernst. *Frederick the Second, 1194–1250*. Translated by E.O. Lorimer. New York: Ungar Press, 1957.

Keen, Maurice. *The Pelican History of Medieval Europe*. London: Penguin, 1982.

Masson, Georgina. *Frederick II of Hohenstaufen*. New York: Secker & Warburg, 1973.

Norwich, John Julius. *A Short History of Byzantium*. New York: Random House, 1999.

Norwich, John Julius. *The Middle Sea*. New York: Doubleday, 2006.

Tyerman, Christopher. *God's War: A New History of the Crusades*. Cambridge, MA: Harvard University Press, 2006.

Van Cleve, T.C. *The Emperor Frederick II of Hohenstaufen*. Oxford: Clarendon Press, 1972.

INDEX

Acknowledgments

Writing this book was a pleasure for this first-time author. It would not have been possible without the help of various friends and associates, whom I would like to thank.

My friends Jerry Goodbody and David Wray read the initial draft. Their comments helped to put me on the right track, which I appreciate. My friend Burks Oakley gave me lots of help with the computer side of writing the book. As I am a confirmed tech idiot, I would not have been able to get any drafts to either the publisher or editor without him.

My thanks to Bruce H. Franklin of Westholme Publishing for guiding a novice through the process of publication. Ron Silverman edited this book, improving it immensely. Thanks for all the help.

All the research for this book was done at the University of Illinois Library and the Champaign Public Library. My thanks to them for their help. Any errors in the text are mine alone.